WAR OF 1812
THE SECOND REVOLUTION

Rainier Chapter
NSDAR

With an Introduction by:
Junius Rochester

Edited by:
Robin Savage

TABLE OF CONTENTS

INTRODUCTION

INTRODUCTION:

The Large Picture:

Did America's War for Independence end with the Treaty of Paris in 1783? Many historians believe that the following twenty years were only a lull, a faux peace, between England and her former colony. The ashes burst into flame again during the administrations of presidents John Adams and Thomas Jefferson, and then became a conflagration after the election of James Madison in 1808. What re-kindled the fire?

Indian and English harassment of Americans in the Old Northwest – our Mid-West – had been an annoyance. Another irritant was the impressment, i.e. arrest, of American seamen by crews of British ships, alleging their prisoners were actually British citizens. Enough was enough. In April of 1812, President Madison sent a message to Congress recommending an immediate 60-day embargo of British goods.

Diplomacy failed. Threats were ignored. Republicans in the U.S. Senate tried to prolong negotiations with Great Britain. In short, events began to out-run cooler heads. Madison was empowered by Congress to call up to 100,000 members of the militia from the states and territories for six months service. The Declaration of War, as composed by President Madison, passed the Senate by 19-13, with New England opposed (they lived off foreign trade). The House supported the War by a vote of 79-49, with the South and West – Thomas Jefferson's precincts – carrying the day.

In 1812- 1815, "Madison's War" included: Naval battles on the Great Lakes; a British blockade of Chesapeake and Delaware bays; American raids in Canada; Britain's humiliating capture and burning of Washington, D.C.; and the emergence of Andrew Jackson ("Old Hickory"), a new American hero, at the Battle of New Orleans. Exhausted, in February 1815, both parties agreed to peace terms at Ghent, Belgium (John Quincy Adams and Albert Gallatin represented the United States). One principle in the peace pact, insisted on by the United States, was *status quo ante bellum,* or restoration of prewar territorial holdings. That restoration of American claims led directly to several episodes affecting the Pacific Northwest.

The Pacific Northwest:

John Jacob Astor was at this time the richest man in America. Before he quadrupled his fortune in Manhattan real estate, Astor's coffers overflowed from the Fur Trade. Pelts – especially the sea otter – were the "soft gold" of the late 1700s. Astor discussed his Pacific commercial interests with Thomas Jefferson, Albert Gallatin, and others. They encouraged him to establish a post at the mouth of the Columbia River. "Oregon" was at that time open country. No nation had asserted her rights to this area, which spread from today's British Columbia to Northern California. An American presence, except for a trading vessel or two, was virtually nonexistent.

After sending two parties westward, one more or less following the 1805-1806 Lewis & Clark trail, the other by sea, the tiny settlement of Astoria was established in 1811. When word of the War of 1812 reached the post in 1813, Astor's partners concluded that their situation was "hopeless." It was decided to abandon the post and return east. This idea met resistance when representatives of the North West Company, a British fur trading outfit, offered to purchase Astoria. Papers were signed and a ship was designated to remove Astor's property and return Sandwich Islander employees to Hawaii.

A British ship, the *Isaac Todd,* was caught in this maelstrom. It had been dispatched to Astoria on March 25, 1813, with supplies for the North West Company at its new, tiny outpost. The *Isaac Todd* was delayed on the coast of Chile, but the twenty-six gun

British warship *Racoon* sailed over the Columbia River bar to take possession of Astoria for Great Britain. Surprise! Astoria was already in British hands, thanks to the North West Company. Astor's Pacific Ocean dream was in shambles and his Far West post had been re-named Fort George.

After the Treaty of Ghent (Christmas, 1915), Astoria once more re-claimed its name and reverted to American ownership. John Jacob Astor lost interest (and a great deal of money) in this enterprise. Other nations had become heavily involved in the Pacific fur trade. The village of Astoria never became the "New York" of the West that Astoria envisaged. The War of 1812 had changed everything.

The Rainier Chapter:

Members of the Rainier Chapter, National Society Daughters of the American Revolution, have taken a close look at the War of 1812. Calling it America's "Second Revolution," members found ancestors who played roles in this strange, almost endless British-American conflict.

Living in the Pacific Northwest does not immunize Americans from the repercussions of the War of 1812 – or from any other national or international event. We are Americans all, and to understand the origins and results of these historical milestones causes us to become informed citizens, fulfilling the dream of Thomas Jefferson and his co-founders.

Junius Rochester
Independent Historian, Seattle, Washington

A NATION'S STORY

OUR NATION'S STORY:

Prelude to War:

August 24, 1814, the unthinkable happens. The White House is in flames; the U.S. Capitol building is a smoldering shell. Three years earlier the House chambers had been completed and the White House had been occupied for only fourteen years. What on earth had happened? The War of 1812 did not start over just one incident or in just a few months; the causes were numerous and some would say inevitable. In fact, the end of the Revolutionary War could be called the beginning of the road to the War of 1812.

On September 3, 1783, the Treaty of Paris was signed ending the conflict between the American Colonists and the British Crown. Even though the treaty acknowledged the United States to be "free, sovereign and independent states", Americans never truly felt secure that Britain would not try to re-impose colonial status on them. In fact, in less than ten years after the signing of the treaty, Britain and the United States were again in negotiations, this time trying to avert another war. Therefore, by 1793, President Washington had chosen John Jay to sail to London. His task was to negotiate a resolution to the issues that had never been truly settled. The resulting "Jay Treaty" was not popular. The "Jeffersonians" tried to block ratification; their main concern was that, if closer ties were established with Britain, it would undercut republicanism. The ensuing debate during ratification initiated a bitter political battle but the Federalist Party was able to get enough votes for it to pass in April of 1796. Again, in 1806, just ten years later, another effort to resolve Issues was tried with the Monroe-Pinkney Treaty. It was an unsuccessful attempt to renew the Jay Treaty. It still did not address the issue of impressment. Consequently, President Jefferson rejected it and refused to send it on to the Senate for ratification, therefore, never going into effect.

Many other contributing factors occurred during the years of Thomas Jefferson's administration. Under Jefferson, stronger ties to France developed. President Jefferson believed that alliances with France could serve to counter Britain's threat to American interests. This, along with the French procurement of Spanish territories in North America, allowed Jefferson an unprecedented opportunity--the Louisiana Purchase. By buying the Territory, Jefferson was able to nearly double the land area of the United States by 800,000 square miles. Moreover, even though Britain was willing to lend to us the $15 million needed for the purchase, the acquisition from France encouraged American expansion west, ultimately adding to the tensions between the two countries.

Other factors beyond America's control were also at work bringing Britain and the United States closer to war. During this time, the Napoleonic Wars raged between Britain and France putting the United States right in the middle. American trade and shipping, the lifeblood of New England, was being greatly affected. American merchantmen and their cargo were being seized as contraband, both sides plundering American shipping interests.

Particularly egregious was the impressment of American sailors by the British Navy. The Chesapeake-Leopard Affair, where the British warship *HMS Leopard* attacked and boarded the American frigate *USS Chesapeake*, was one of the most egregious acts, and incensed the American public. On June 22, 1807, when the *Leopard* pursued, attacked, and boarded the *Chesapeake*, four American crewmembers were seized and tried for desertion from the British Navy; one was hanged. Americans were infuriated and demanded retribution. In a desperate attempt to avert war and appease the citizenry, Jefferson turned to an embargo on all foreign trade, it was an economic disaster.

American ships were attacked, boarded, then searched for sailors to impress.

Exports fell from $108 million in 1807 to $22 million within one year. Farm prices plummeted. New England shipping was destroyed, hundreds of ships sat idle and nearly 30,000 sailors were jobless. And, by early 1809, Congress was forced to repeal the Embargo Act for a new tactic--"The Non-Intercourse Act".

This new "embargo" reopened trade with all of Europe except Britain and France. It helped to relieve the economic issue the previous embargo had caused but still did nothing to stop the seizures of American ships and seamen. Within a year, Congress tried again to find a solution and repealed the Non-Intercourse Act replacing it with Macon's Bill No. 2, another attempt to get America's neutrality recognized by both the French and the English. Finally, something that was partially effective. France immediately repealed the French restrictions on American trade. Nevertheless, Napoleon's willingness to capitulate was due only to the fact that he saw it as an opportunity to cripple Britain economically; he was right, it worked. For over a year and a half the only European country not trading with America was Great Britain, which caused food shortages, unemployment and a backlog of unsold goods at British ports. In desperation, the British Parliament finally ended their restrictions on American trade and their onerous policy of impressment but it was too late, the seeds of war had been sown.

Grievances:

"Never did a prisoner, released from his chains, feel such relief as I shall on shaking off the shackles of power." This statement from Thomas Jefferson in a letter to his friend P. S. Dupont de Nemours sums up the frustration Jefferson felt over his failure to ensure America's sovereignty on the high seas. Not treaties, embargos nor diplomacy had worked and one would truly believe that Jefferson was sincere when he stated, "I shall look on my friends still buffeting the storm, with anxiety indeed, but not with envy." Moreover, a "buffeting storm" is exactly what James Madison inherited as he took over the presidency from Jefferson.

On Saturday, March 4, 1809, Madison took the oath of office as the fourth President of the United States, not knowing that he would be the first American president to declare war. However, just fifteen months later he would send a letter—later dubbed "Madison's War Message"—to both houses of Congress requesting just that, a declaration of war against Great Britain. Madison, also known as "Little Jemmy" or "His Little Majesty" by his detractors, was the main architect of the Constitution. At only five foot three and one-hundred pounds, what he lacked in physical stature he made up in intellectual brilliance; thus, his skills at oratory helped convince the Senate to approve a declaration of war by only 19 yea votes to 13 nays.

"British cruisers have been in the continued practice of violating the American flag on the great highway of nations, and of seizing and carrying off persons sailing under it… thousands of American citizens, under the safeguard of public law and of their national flag, have been torn from their country and from everything dear to them".

Madison listed the impressment of American sailors by the British Royal Navy as the first and foremost of the grievances. As Britain did not recognize the process of renouncing citizenship – "once an Englishman, always an Englishman", they felt justified to stop and board any ship that might have an English "deserter" onboard. This often amounted to impressing any able-bodied English-speaking man whether he was born in England or not. To counter this practice, the American government provided seamen with documents attesting to their American citizenship but these papers were largely ignored by the British, resulting in about 1,300 of the sailors of the approximately 5,000 men impressed, being American born.

"British cruisers have been in the practice also of violating the rights and the peace of our coasts...and have wantonly spilt American blood within the sanctuary of our territorial jurisdiction...our commerce has been plundered in every sea, the great staples of our country have been cut off from their legitimate markets, and a destructive blow aimed at our agricultural and maritime interests."

The second main grievance was the British blockade of American trade to France during the Napoleonic Wars. England, in her effort to hobble Napoleon's economy, put a naval stranglehold on the much needed supplies going to France, allowing only vessels that had first passed through a British port to sail unimpeded. As a neutral country, the United States felt that this was an unprecedented assault on America's sovereignty.

"In reviewing the conduct of Great Britain toward the United States our attention is necessarily drawn to the warfare just renewed by the savages on one of our extensive frontiers — a warfare which is known to spare neither age nor sex and to be distinguished by features peculiarly shocking to humanity."

Surprisingly, only one paragraph within a twenty-one paragraph document mentions the Indian raids on American settlements in the Northwest Territories. The settlers, who had flooded into the new "Promised Land" after the Revolutionary War, were sure that the British authorities who had refused to relinquish their military posts on US soil were using those posts to supply the Indian nations with the support and means to carry out raids on the new American settlements. As war loomed, Maj. Gen. Isaac Brock, the British commander of Upper Canada (modern Ontario), sought to augment his meager regular and Canadian militia forces with Indian allies, thereby providing the only proof American settlers needed to confirm their suspicion of British incitement and provocation. In fact, it had only been seven months prior to Madison's "War Message" that the Shawnee Confederacy, whose leader was Tecumseh, had been defeated at the Battle of Tippecanoe by Henry Harrison, forcing Tecumseh, his brother Tenskwatawa, and the remaining Shawnees to flee into Canada.

An American cartoon attacking the alliance between the "Humane British" and the Indians during the War of 1812.
Library of Congress, Washington, D.C.

"Whether the United States shall continue passive under these progressive usurpations and these accumulating wrongs, or, opposing force to force in defense of their national rights, shall commit a just cause into the hands of the Almighty Disposer of Events…I am happy in the assurance that the decision will be worthy the enlightened and patriotic councils of a virtuous, a free, and a powerful nation." No more prophetic words could have been penned for, on June 18, 1812, Congress vote "Yeah" and Mr. Madison had his war.

Bitter Opposition:

By June 18, 1812, America was again at war with Great Britain and not all were happy about it. In fact, the main reason for going to war was, ironically, no longer an issue. Two days earlier, the British foreign minister had announced that the Orders in Council, which allowed the seizure of American ships and impressment of American sailors, was to be repealed. So to say that Americans were "mixed" in their attitudes toward going to war would be an understatement. New England, the richest section in the country, bitterly opposed the war and interfered with its progress by withholding both money and troops. The main consensus in New England was "If the people of the West and the South wanted to fight, then let them pay for the war".

The cost of the Revolutionary War had been $37 million at the national level plus an additional $114 million debt for the states. There was little money in the treasury and even President Madison's own party members had reservations. Congressman Hermanus Bleecker's concerns were stated eloquently when he said, "It is impossible that we can go to war when the embargo ends, sixty days from now. Where are our armies? Our navy? Have we the money to fight a war? Why, it would be treason to go to war this soon, so poorly prepared." Although the many concerns were valid, the "War Hawks" led by Henry Clay, Speaker of the House, and John C. Calhoun were able to prevail. No matter what New England did, Clay and Calhoun were certain that the rest of the country believed in "the cause". Surely, their beliefs that the public supported the war were vindicated when one month later the riots in Baltimore violently proved their point.

For five weeks, the Federalist Printer Alexander Contee Hanson had been publishing tirades against Madison in his newspaper *"The Federal Republican"*. On July 26, 1812, Hanson and his supporters had been locked in the Baltimore City Jail, "for their own protection". That next night an anti-Federalist mob gathered

The Conspiracy Against Baltimore/The War Dance at Montgomery Court House. Engraving. 1812.

outside the jail and, with help, was able to break into the cells holding Hanson and his fellow Federalists. While they were dragging Hanson and his supporters into the streets, the mob was heard singing, “We'll feather and tar every dammed Tory, and this is the way for American glory”. A surviving victim of the attack, John Thompson, later related his experience. “I had left my coat in the gaol, and they tore my shirt and other clothing, and put the tar on my bare body, upon which they put feathers. They drew me along in the cart in this condition, calling me traitor and tory and other scandalous names.” Many Federalists were attacked and tortured that night. Two of the more famous victims set upon were Revolutionary War heroes: General Henry “Light Horse Harry” Lee and General James M. Lingan who died later that night from his wounds.

No matter which side you were on, Americans would soon realize that of all the dissent against the war Congressman Bleecker’s would be the most prophetical of them all.

Impotency:

Congressman Bleecker's concerns about the readiness of the United States to go to war were well founded. Besides the question about funding a war; the actual strength of the Regular Army in June 1812 totaled approximately 11,744 officers and men, including an estimated 5,000 recruits that had enlisted since that preceding January. This was in contrast to the 35,600 that Congress had authorized, making the Regular Army's size a little more than one third of what Congress wanted or needed. The Navy consisted of fewer than 20 seagoing vessels: three large 44-gun frigates, 3 smaller frigates of the *Constellation* class carrying 38 guns and 14 other ships even smaller with fewer guns than the *Constellation* class frigates. The Army consisted of small military units scattered around the country and were more of a constabulary force than a fighting force. No wonder the British considered the Americans as an enemy "unworthy of serious regard".

Even with a military disadvantage, the "War Hawks" in Congress expected a short war. The plan was to make a rapid expansion into Canada where the inhabitants "under the British yoke" would welcome the American Army with open arms as "liberators". They were welcomed with arms all right: British Brown Bess's and 5.50 Howitzers and, due to unpreparedness and lack of leadership, the plan to "liberate" Canada was an abysmal failure.

On July 12, 1812, General William Hull led the first American invasion into British North America, occupying the town of Sandwich; he issued this proclamation:

> INHABITANTS OF CANADA
>
> After thirty years of peace and prosperity, the United States have been driven to arms. The injuries and aggressions, the insults and indignities of Great Britain have once more left no alternative but manly resistance or unconditional submission. The army under

> my command has invaded your country. The standard of the union now waves over the territory of Canada. To the peaceful and unoffending inhabitants it brings neither danger nor difficulty. I come to find enemies, not to make them; I come to protect not to injure you ... I have a force which will break down all opposition, and that force is but the vanguard of a much greater. If, contrary to your own interest, and the just expectations of my country, you should take part in the approaching contest, you will be considered and treated as enemies, and the horrors and calamities of war will stalk you...

While General Hull waited for the Canadian inhabitants "under the British yoke" to join him, a small troop of 45 British regulars, 180 Canadian Voygeurs and 400 Indians attacked Fort Michilimackinac. The American Commander, Lieutenant Porter Hanks, was amazed to see the British at his door; his first response was "War! What war?" Washington D.C. had failed to warn the outlying military posts that they had declared war on Britain! Lieutenant Hanks had no other choice but to surrender. A few days later, emboldened by the news of Fort Michilimackinac's bloodless surrender, a band of Indians allied with the Britain surrounded Fort Dearborn (present day Chicago). Captain Nathan Heald, with only 50 men under his command and greatly outnumbered, decided to negotiate an agreement for safe passage in exchange for trade goods. On the morning of August 15, Captain Heald, his soldiers, a handful of militia, and the local settlers with their families set out for Fort Wayne; it was an ambush. Men, women, and children were massacred; the few survivors told of fellow Americans "lying naked with principally all their heads cut off"; 86 souls were brutally killed that day.

The horrendous news of Fort Michilimackinac and Dearborn reached General Hull causing him to panic and retreat back to Fort Detroit. By August 16, the British and their Indian allies, led by Tecumseh, had crossed the Detroit River and were advancing on the fort. General Hull, apparently in a terror-induced state of paralysis, surrenders the fort, over 2,000 men, 30 cannon, 300 rifles, 2,500 muskets and the only armed American vessel on the Upper Lakes, the brig *Adams*. This was not only a total embarrassment for the army and President Madison, but also for the American people. For his unacceptable actions, General Hull was court martialed; he ended up facing three charges of treason, four counts of cowardice, and seven counts of neglect of duty and conduct unbecoming an officer. He was sentenced to hang. President Madison later commuted his sentence.

For the rest of 1812 and 1813 American attempts to invade British North America continued to be unsuccessful. A series of battles from the Battle for Queenston Heights to the Siege of Fort Meigs to the Battle of Fort Stephenson were either defeats or short-lived victories. The only true bright spots against the British were during the skirmishes at sea. Badly out-manned and out gunned by the Royal Navy, the Congress had enlisted the services of the merchant class as privateers to bolster the number of American vessels involved in the conflict. By using privateers to harass British merchant vessels, it not only caused financial hardship but it also helped keep the British Royal Navy somewhat occupied, allowing the much smaller United States Navy to determine the time and place for an attack on British naval vessels.

On August 19, 1812, the USS Constitution caught site of the large mainsail of the British frigate "Guerriere". The Guerriere was known for being a notorious "impressment ship" and a prize that Captain Isaac Hull of the Constitution was not going to lose. During the ensuing battle, the crew of the USS Constitution was amazed at how the cannon fire from the British guns seemed to bounce off the Constitution's tough oak sides, thereby winning her the nickname "Old Ironsides".

Action between USS Constitution and HMS Guerriere, 19 August 1812

The battle lasted only 2 hours before the Guerriere was forced to surrender. Winning a battle against a "ship-of-the-line", her capture became a symbol of American honor, perseverance and pride.

The battle between the USS Constitution and the HMS Guerriere was not the only naval victory for the United States. On September 10, 1813, the Battle of Lake Erie was fought. Even after Commodore Oliver Hazzard Perry lost his flag ship, the Lawrence, and had to abandon her for the Niagara, Commodore Perry with only nine small vessels outmaneuvered and outflanked a squadron of six much larger British ships. After the victory, Perry, in his report to General William Henry Harrison, pens his most famous line: "We have met the enemy and they are ours!" This victory not only assured American control of Lake Erie for the remainder of the war but it also helped to assure the retaking of Detroit and the win at the Battle of the Thames. The British defeat at the hands of General William Henry Harrison was not only considered a pivotal American win but with the death of Tecumseh, it also assured the end of the Indian confederation that had allied themselves with the British.

Some might say that it was a miracle that the United States had not already lost the war long before Battle of the Thames was even fought. However, there were other factions at work that had kept the full force of Britain's might occupied. Without the distraction called the Napoleonic Wars, the "Second Revolution" would have been the end for the young nation called the United States of America.

Britain's Preoccupation:

Americans saw the War of 1812 as a matter of survival. If they lost, it would be the loss of their liberty, freedom, and sovereignty; for the British, it was seen as a nuisance. Britain's main military objective was to repel any invasion of their holdings in North America and then to maintain it until they were able to defeat Napoleon. After that, they would turn their attention to the upstart Americans and take care of them once and for all.

Britain's conflict with France started as early as 1793 with the War of the First Coalition. The monarchs of Europe began to worry that the political and social changes brought about by the American and French Revolutions would grow and overrun their own realms. The War of the First Coalition was an attempt by the dynastic powers of Europe to reverse the outcome of the French Revolution and restore the French monarchy. The first Coalition included Austria, Prussia, Great Britain, Spain, Sardinia, and the Netherlands, which was pretty much a disaster for both Austria and Prussia. By the end of the War of the First Coalition, France had gained Belgium, the Tyrol, and most of Italy.

By 1798, the tenuous treaty signed in 1797 failed and the War of the Second Coalition commenced. This Coalition again included Austria and Great Britain, with Russia, Portugal, the Ottoman Empire, and the Kingdom of Naples also joining. After a devastating defeat, Russia pulled out, then Austria and finally, by 1802, only Britain was left. After a failed attack in Holland, Great Britain was also forced to capitulate. This peace did not last any longer than the previous one.

In 1805 the War of the Third Coalition, this time including Britain, Russia, Austria, and Sweden, broke out. In less than a year, Austria was again defeated and they were forced out of the Coalition. Shortly thereafter, the Coalition was reformed, this

History map of Central Europe 1805-1807: Wars of Third Coalition

time with Prussia and without Austria. The crushing defeat of Prussia at the Battle of Jena crumbled the fourth Coalition. So by 1808, Napoleon was master of all central Europe and was now to turn his attention to the Iberian Peninsula.

The Peninsular War started when France turned on its ally Spain removing King Charles IV and replacing the Spanish King with Joseph Bonaparte, Napoleon's brother. This action infuriated the Spanish people who started a resistance movement later known as the Guerilla War. The Spanish Guerillas were able to wear down Napoleon's forces by using up valuable supplies, cutting off units and often overwhelming them with guerilla tactics that were previously unknown in warfare. This allowed Great Britain to develop a foothold on the Continent and, with the help of Portugal, develop a western front against the French forces. Around this time, Napoleon made one of his worst military decisions, which was to invade Russia. Why he would decide to split his forces and create an eastern front is unknown but on June 12, 1812, the Grande Armée crossed into Russia.

For months, the Russian Army withdrew, burning everything as they retreated in a vain attempt to slow down Napoleon's advance. Finally, on September 7, the two armies faced each other near Moscow in the Battle of Borodino. The battle was the largest engagement of the Napoleonic War, involving almost a quarter of a million troops. The French took the battlefield and entered Moscow but the Russians would not give up. They had learned from the Spanish about guerilla tactics; they released criminals from the prisons and burned whatever they could. Napoleon was trapped. He was harassed by Russian peasants and irregulars, had no way to replace his lost troops, and was quickly running out of supplies with winter quickly approaching. He was

Circa 1814 cartoon of Napoleon's exile to Elba.

forced to retreat. By November, Napoleon was left with only 27,000 fit soldiers; he had lost some 380,000 men and 100,000 of them had been captured. This was the beginning of the end. By April 1814, Napoleon was forced to sign the Treaty of Fontainebleau and he was exiled to Elba.

If Napoleon had not kept Great Britain occupied in Europe, America's declaration of war in 1812 would have been a very short-lived endeavor and the outcome would have been drastically different. As it was, it still gave Britain the opportunity to "teach the Americans a lesson", one that would be remembered as the worst attack on the American mainland until the Twin Towers on September 11, 2001.

Conflagration:

La Grande Armée of France is defeated, the Treaty of Fontainebleau has been signed and Napoleon is safely exiled to the Island of Elba. It is now time for Britain to shift her attention to the bothersome American situation. Most British see the Americans as a "nest of pirates" for using privateers. The British Army and Royal Navy see them as inferior rabble that they will give "a complete drubbing to". No wonder, after hearing of the defeat of Napoleon, Captain Joseph Nicholson wrote to the Secretary of the Navy, "We should have to fight hereafter, not for free trade and sailor's rights, not for the conquest of Canada, but for our national existence..."

If American merchants thought the British blockade before April 1814 was onerous then they were in for a rude awakening. Once the Royal Navy was free to turn its full force against the United States, the blockade became literally impenetrable. The British were able to raid all along the Chesapeake at will, burning as they went. They encountered little resistance as most of America's regular army was on the Canadian border, basically leaving the militias to defend the rest of the country. In addition, Vice Admiral Sir Alexander Cochrane, the admiral in command of the expeditionary forces in the Chesapeake campaign, hated Americans. He allowed his troops to pillage, what they could not carry off, he let them torch. His distain was apparent when he stated, "like naughty spaniels...they should be treated with great severity before you can even make them tractable." Thus, with this attitude, 5,000 British troops landed at Benedict, Maryland.

On August 19, 1814, John Armstrong, Secretary of War, hears of the landing at Benedict. He is so sure that Major General Robert Ross' objective is Baltimore, Maryland that he does little to set up defenses for Washington, D.C. Due to Armstrong's lack of action, President Madison just a month earlier had created the 10th Military District and had appointed General William Winder as Commander of both the defenses of Washington and Baltimore. However, this is not enough time to prepare and, due to the lack of logistical support from Secretary Armstrong, General Winder is unable to muster more than 500 regulars, forcing him to rely heavily on militia. Therefore, on August 24, 1814, General Winder, woefully unprepared, takes a final stand against General Ross at the Battle of Bladensburg with devastating results. In fact, the American line's retreat is later dubbed "The Bladensburg Races". Charles Ball, a free black, pretty much sums up the outcome, "our militia ran like sheep chased by dogs", the speed of the retreat was such that the British lost men to heat stroke just trying to keep up with the fleeing Americans.

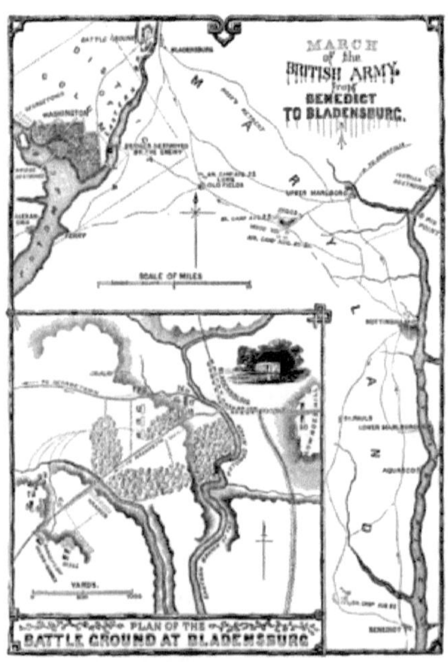

Map of the campaign and battlefield of Bladensburg, from Benjamin J. Lossing's *Pictorial Field Book of the War of 1812*

The path was now open to the Capitol and General Ross' troops marched with revenge on their minds, driven on by the memory of the American's burning of the parliament building at York. As word of the approaching British reaches Washington, panic ensues. As President Madison has already left the Capitol to meet General Winder, it is left up to his wife Dolley and a clerk of the Treasury Department, Stephen Pleasonton, to save the important papers and documents of the government. While Pleasonton collected the still unpublished secret journals of Congress, the commission and correspondence of George Washington, the Articles of Confederation, and the United States Constitution, Mrs. Madison is at the White House packing up what she can to transport out of the city. Her letter to her sister describes the dire situation:

My husband left me yesterday morning to join General Winder. He inquired anxiously whether I had courage or firmness to remain in the President's house until his return on the morrow or succeeding day, and on my assurance that I had no fear but for him and the success of our army, he left beseeching me to take care of myself and of the Cabinet papers, public and private. I have since received two dispatches from him, written with a pencil. The last is alarming, because he desires I should be ready at a moment's warning to enter my carriage, and leave the city; that the enemy seemed stronger than had at first been reported, and it might happen that they would reach the city with the intention of destroying it. I am accordingly ready; I have pressed as many Cabinet papers into trunks as to fill one carriage; our private property must be sacrificed, as it is impossible to procure wagons for its transportation. I am determined not to go myself until I see Mr. Madison safe, so that he can accompany me, as I hear of much hostility towards him. Disaffection stalks around us. My friends and acquaintances are all gone, even Colonel C. with his hundred, who were stationed as a guard in this enclosure. French John (a faithful servant), with his usual activity and resolution, offers to spike the cannon at the gate, and lay a train of powder, which would blow up the British, should they enter the house. To the last proposition I positively object, without being able to make him understand why all advantages in war may not be taken.

Wednesday Morning, twelve o'clock. -- Since sunrise I have been turning my spy-glass in every direction, and watching with unwearied anxiety, hoping to discover the approach of my dear husband and his friends; but, alas! I can descry only groups of military, wandering in all directions, as if there was a lack of arms, or of spirit to fight for their own fireside.

Three o'clock. -- Will you believe it, my sister? we have had a battle, or skirmish, near Bladensburg, and here I am still, within sound of the cannon! Mr. Madison comes not. May

God protect us! Two messengers, covered with dust, come to bid me fly; but here I mean to wait for him... At this late hour a wagon has been procured, and I have had it filled with plate and the most valuable portable articles, belonging to the house. Whether it will reach its destination, the "Bank of Maryland," or fall into the hands of British soldiery, events must determine. Our kind friend, Mr. Carroll, has come to hasten my departure, and in a very bad humor with me, because I insist on waiting until the large picture of General Washington is secured, and it requires to be unscrewed from the wall. This process was found too tedious for these perilous moments; I have ordered the frame to be broken, and the canvas taken out. It is done! and the precious portrait placed in the hands of two gentlemen of New York, for safe keeping. And now, dear sister, I must leave this house, or the retreating army will make me a prisoner in it by filling up the road I am directed to take. When I shall again write to you, or where I shall be to-morrow, I cannot tell!

On August 24, 1814, with only 4,000 troops, Major General Robert Ross marches into Washington D.C., and there is no resistance. After a mock legislative session where the British "voted" to burn the city, the two buildings housing the Senate and House, along with the Library of Congress, are set aflame. The invaders then set their sights on the President's House and head northwest. Finding the table already set for dinner, they gorge themselves, after which General Ross drinks a toast to "Little Jemmy" and orders the torching of the White House. Not finished, the Navy Yard is targeted as well as the building housing the newspaper the *National Intelligencer*, which had branded their commander, Vice Admiral Cockburn, "The Ruffian".

British Troops in **Washington** courtesy Library of Congress

The government is in disarray, the troops are scattered, the President has fled across the Potomac River into Virginia. There is nothing anyone can do as they watch Washington burn. However, as if on cue the "The Hurricane of Providence" arrives, bringing staggering winds and incredible lightning with roaring thunder. Most of the city's public buildings have been burned, there is no shelter left and as the ensuing tornado approaches, the invaders are trapped. In less than 15 minutes, Mother Nature has done what all of America could not, devastate the British line. Unable to take cover they are thrown around like rag dolls, their cannons are thrown in the air, and then the torrential rains start. For two hours, it is a deluge, dousing the flames and sending the British scurrying back to their ships.

The next day President Madison quickly returns to Washington where he and Dolley survey the destruction but there is no time for mourning. The City of Baltimore and, more importantly, the whole country are in jeopardy.

Turning Point:

"Good God! How have we been disgraced?" This was not just the sentiment of Captain Joseph Nicholson; it was how every American felt on hearing of the defeat at Bladensburg and the burning of Washington. The disaster of the Capitol was devastating but it did the opposite of what the British intended. Instead of crushing the will of the citizens to fight, it rallied them. "Every American heart is bursting with shame and indignation at the catastrophe... All hearts and hands have cordially united in the common cause. Every day, almost every hour, bodies of troops are marching in to our assistance..." George Douglas was right in his observation. In just a few weeks, more than 10,000 volunteers had poured into Baltimore to help in her defense and she would need them.

Major General Samuel Smith is chosen as the overall commander to defend Baltimore; he knew that the British offensive would come in a combined sea/land attack. He therefore appointed General John Stricker as commander of the land forces and Major George Armistead as commander of Fort Henry. The two commanders wasted no time. General Stricker immediately called for all able-bodied men to erect earth works around Baltimore. Major Armistead called for merchants to scuttle their own ships in the channel between Lazaretto Battery and Fort McHenry, and the citizens of Baltimore answered the call. In less than three weeks, three miles of earth works are built and 22 ships are scuttled and sunk. It was just in time. For on September 12, 1814, General Robert Ross and his troops land at North Point to begin the 12-mile trek to Baltimore.

Major Armistead knows that Fort Henry is going to be mercilessly bombarded by the combined firepower of at least 19 ships of the line. The scuttled merchant ships will keep the British out of the Patapsco River but will the Fort and his men be able to stand up to the onslaught? Whether they prevail or not, all depends upon the moral of the defenders and what would inspire them more than "a flag so large that the British would have no difficulty seeing it from a distance"? Therefore, a local flag maker named Mary Pickersgilde is commissioned to sew the biggest flag in the country. Its final dimensions are 30 x 42 feet, which takes her seven assistants and her six weeks to complete. She is paid only $574.44 for the task. She finishes it just in time. As General Ross lands at North Point, Vice Admiral Alexander Cochrane sails up the Patapsco River right towards Fort McHenry.

Bombardment of **Fort McHenry** during War of **1812**

As General Ross' troops progress towards Baltimore, they encounter a small force of American troops sent out to delay the British advance. As General Ross rides up to access the situation, he is mortally wounded by a sniper's bullet; his last order is to relinquish his command to Colonel Arthur Brooke. Even though Brooke is able to beat back the American attack, it is devastating to the British: 46 men are killed, 300 are wounded and the commander of their land forces is lost. Meanwhile, from a position of over 2 miles away, Admiral Cochrane has commenced the attack on Fort Henry. After five or more hours of bombardment, he draws closer believing that the damage he has wrought has crippled the Fort's defenses. It is a bad move. Major Armistead responds with an order of such intense returning fire that the British fleet is pushed back to their original location.

Even with the loss of General Ross, Colonel Brooke continues the British advance. However, as his front line gets close to Baltimore, they come face to face with the newly constructed fortifications. To attack they will have to cross two miles of open field and ford a steep-banked creek before they even reach the enemy who, being protected by earth works, would have unfettered ability to fire at will. Brooke decides against a frontal attack on the American defenses, coming up with another plan. He will have the Royal Marines make a nighttime diversionary raid on the south end of Hampstead Hill, thus diverting attention so he can launch a silent bayonet attack on the northeast side. American forces spot the Royal Marines, they are not able to land and the plot is thwarted; Colonel Brooke is forced to retreat.

Meanwhile, Admiral Cochrane continued the bombardment of Fort McHenry. Before the barrage subsides, 1,500 190-pound bombs, 1,800 to 2,000 shells, and 700 to 800 rockets will be launched at the American stronghold. In dread, the citizens of Baltimore watched the spectacle from their rooftops, not knowing if Fort McHenry had surrendered or not. Only the explosions of the rockets and the occasional lightening flash illuminated the skies for, earlier that night, they had extinguished all lights so as not to provide a reference for the British gunners. Not only was Baltimore dark but all lights at Fort McHenry had also been extinguished as the defenders did not want to provide any additional advantage to the British. Just hours earlier there had been a direct hit on their powder magazine and, only by the grace of God, the shell had failed to explode.

As the sun begins to rise on September 14, 1814, all eyes are on the Fort including a young Georgetown attorney named Francis Scott Key. He had boarded one of the British ships to negotiate the release of a friend who was currently being held as a prisoner of war. Not allowed to leave before the attack, he was unable to do anything but watch from the deck

Francis Scott Key

of the British ship, HMS Tonnant. As dawn approached and the fog lifted, he was able to make out the American flag still flying above the Fort. The sight of his county's flag still flying in defiance inspired him to write the poem "Defense of Fort McHenry" which later became the "Star Spangled Banner", our National Anthem.

After the retreat from Baltimore by Colonel Brooke and the inability to destroy Fort McHenry, Vice Admiral Cochrane reluctantly made the decision to suspend the Chesapeake campaign and, as the Royal Navy lifted anchor and set sail, the Americans realized they had successfully defended their country against the world's mightiest military power. Private Isaac Monroe writes to a friend of the jubilant celebration, "At dawn on the 14th, our morning gun was fired, the flag hoisted, Yankee Doodle played, and we all appeared in full view of a formidable and mortified enemy, who had calculated upon our surrender in 20 minutes after the commencement of the action." It was a turning point in the war and a major catalyst in pressuring Britain to negotiate for peace.

Treaty of Ghent:

By the summer of 1814, President Madison's political troubles were beginning to affect the war effort almost as much as the military disasters had. The New England states had never been in support of the war and the Federalists, who were the political power in the northeast, are becoming more and more antagonistic in their opposition. The general rule among the governors of New England was to provide as little support in money and materials as possible and, with only one exception, they ignored all requests to call up their state militias. Madison, in retaliation, cut off federal payments to any state militias that refused to obey direct orders from the War Department. The tensions between the President, a Democratic-Republican, and the Eastern governors, Federalists, came to a boiling point when five New England states called for a convention to outline their grievances against the Federal government.

Late in 1814, representatives from Connecticut, Massachusetts, New Hampshire, Rhode Island, and Vermont convened at the Old State House in Hartford, Connecticut. By holding the meetings in secret, it only gave credence to the rumor that the convention was being convened expressly to discuss succession. In fact, Madison was so concerned about the possibility that he pulled troops from the Canadian border to head south to Albany in preparation to exert federal authority of necessary. His concerns were justified since Massachusetts' Governor Caleb Strong had already sent an envoy to Britain to discuss an agreement for a separate peace treaty. However, by the conclusion of the Hartford Convention, calmer heads had prevailed and the talk of succession was not included among the Conventions resolutions, which were:

1. The prohibition of any trade embargo lasting over 60 days;
2. The requirement of a two-thirds Congressional majority to declare war, admit a new state, or impose any interdiction on foreign commerce;

3. The removal of the three-fifths representation advantage of the South;
4. To limit Presidents to one term;
5. To require each subsequent President to be from a different state than his predecessor.

The Federalists were not Madison's only concern. Earlier attempts at a peace agreement had failed and the President was worried that the victory at Baltimore would not be enough for America to negotiate from strength. As early as 1813, Czar Nicholas I had tried to broker a peace deal; war between the United States and Britain hampered Russian trade with America and distracted Britain from the fight against Napoleon. Nonetheless, even though Madison was willing to have Russia broker the talks, the British were not; it would be over another year before London was willing to come to the table. Finally, by early 1814, Britain felt that they were ready to negotiate from strength. Their wins in the Northwest Territories had garnered them new holdings around the Great Lakes whereas the Americans had lost land. Therefore, in January of that year, Britain's foreign minister Lord Castlereagh offered to negotiate directly with the United States.

Even though both sides' ultimate goal was to end the war, their initial terms for peace were far apart. Britain wanted *uti possidetis,* where both sides would keep what they had won during the conflict. America wanted status quo ante bellum, where everything would be restored to its status before the war. Another major sticking point was the issue of the native peoples. The British wanted parts of the State of Ohio and the Territories of Indiana and Michigan to be used to create a "Native Territory"; this would create a buffer between British North America and any future American expansion.

As negotiations dragged on, the American defeat at Bladensburg and the burning of Washington gave negotiating strength to the British. When the British invasion of Baltimore was unsuccessful, the negotiating advantage shifted to the Americans.

Each side was so rooted to their position and the advantage shifted so readily that the likelihood that one or both sides would break off negotiations was always a possibility. However, on Christmas Eve 1814, after almost a year of talks, the Treaty of Ghent is signed. America gets what she wants, status quo ante bellum. The eleven articles of peace state that everything would be as it was before, as if no treasure has been lost, no blood had been spilt nor any capitols were burnt. However, just because the Treaty of Ghent is signed does not mean it is over. More blood will be spilled and more men will lose their lives before news of peace reaches America 3,000 miles away.

Great Britain and The United States Signing a Peace Treaty at Ghent

The Final Battle:

Both the Americans and the British know that their current military position will affect their bargaining power during negotiations at Ghent, and now the British retreat at Baltimore has given a potential advantage to the Americans. Therefore, after Admiral Cochrane's inability to take control of the Chesapeake, a new strategy is tried, the taking of the Mississippi River and control of the Louisiana Territory. By defeating the American forces at New Orleans and moving up the Mississippi Valley, the British southern forces would be able to join with the northern troops from Canada and surround the United States. As Lord Castlereagh, the architect of the Louisiana invasion put it, they would be "...little better than prisoners in their own country."

While Britain is preparing its forces for New Orleans, the American southern campaign is focused on southern Alabama and Georgia, as well as northern Florida. Commanded by Major General Andrew Jackson, the southern military forces have been concentrating on defeating the northern Creek Nation, also known as the "Red Sticks". As they had in the Ohio River Valley, Britain had encouraged the southeastern Indian tribes to wage war on the American settlers diverting American military resources away from direct conflict with British troops, thereby weakening their forces and limiting their ability to fight on multiple fronts. By late September of 1814, General Jackson had subdued the Creek Nation and on August 9, the Treaty of Fort Jackson was signed, ceding 1.9 million acres of Creek and Cherokee lands to the United States. Jackson is now able to focus his attention directly on the British.

General Andrew Jackson's hatred for the British was well known. His whole family had fought for independence in the Revolutionary War and had suffered greatly at the hands of the British. By the time Jackson had reached the age of 13 years, he had already enlisted in the North Carolina militia, had been held captive by the British and had been wounded in the face by a British officer's saber. In less than a year both brothers were dead and his mother, having been forced to nurse British soldiers, died after contracting cholera. By age 14, Jackson was an orphan. From that time forward, he would have a burning hatred for the British whom he blamed for the loss of his family.

On December 2, 1814, General Jackson entered New Orleans. He immediately started on plans for the defenses around the city and the recruitment of volunteers. He called on everyone to assist, regulars and militia, merchants and pirates, Indians and free blacks; everyone was called upon to defend the city. His oratory was rousing, "Who are we? And for what are we going to fight? Are we the titled slaves of George III? The military conscripts of Napoleon the Great? Or the frozen peasants of the Russian Czar? No. We are the free born sons of America. The citizens of the only republic now existing in the world. And the only people on earth who possess rights, liberties, and property which they *dare* call their own." Within days, he had enlisted over 4,000 volunteers, some coming from as far as Kentucky.

While the Americans were preparing, the British were waiting, waiting for cooler weather, waiting for their new army commander, waiting as they mulled over their battle plans. The British did not seem to be worried at all; in fact, they were so confident that their flag would be flying over "the Crown Colony of New Orleans" that they had a complete civil government board the flagship in preparation to rule over their new territories. It seems that their biggest concern about delaying the invasion was the boredom the men might

Army placements near New Orleans

incur. However, due to the death of Major General Ross at Baltimore, a replacement was needed to command the land forces and they had been ordered to wait for his replacement, Major General Edward Pakenham, who would rendezvous with the fleet in Jamaica. Nonetheless, Admiral Cochrane disobeyed orders and decided to set sail without Pakenham. He would eventually come to regret that decision.

On December 12, 1814, the large British fleet anchors east of Lake Borgne where they encountered a small American flotilla of only five gunboats intent upon blocking their access to Lakes Borgne and Pontchartrain. It was a rout, in less than an hour the British navy had killed 6 Americans, wounded 35, and captured the remaining 86, which allowed them to establish a garrison on Pea Island where they create a base of operations. By the day before Christmas Eve the British are ready; they send a vanguard of 1,800 soldiers up the Mississippi River and reach Lacoste Plantation, only 9 miles south of the city. However, General John Keane decides not to proceed; he calls for his men to make encampment and waits for reinforcements. This is not a good move on Keane's part. Jackson is enraged, stating, "By the Eternal, they shall not sleep on our soil." That evening he leads 2,131 men on a raid against the British encampment killing 46, wounding 167, with 67 reported missing. Even though the British are able to hold their position, the raid gives the defenders more time to shore up their fortifications, which will become a defining factor five days later.

The Battle of New Orleans, by Edward Percy Moran, 1910

Finally, on Christmas Day, Major General Edward Pakenham arrives; he immediately starts preparation for a full-scale attack on the American fortifications and early morning on January 8, 1815, the order is given, "Attack!". The two-pronged assault floundered from the start. The 85th

Regiment, commanded by Colonel William Thornton, took longer than anticipated to cross the Mississippi, not even starting the crossing until just before daybreak, putting them 12 hours behind schedule. The 44th East Essex Regiment of Foot, commanded by Colonel Thomas Mullins, forget the ladders and fascines that are needed to cross the canal and scale the earthworks. Even Mother Nature was against them. Heavy fog had blanketed the land until just before the British approached the American defenses when it suddenly lifted, exposing the advancing line to devastating artillery fire. By the time it was over, General Pakenham, General Gibbs, and General Keane were either killed or wounded along with most of the senior officers with the British incurred over 2,000 casualties in contrast to the 71 Americans lost.

On February 5, 1815, New Orleanians watched as the British Royal Navy sailed away, marking the end of the last major battle of the War of 1812 and the last time an invading army from Britain would set foot on American soil.

Manifest Destiny:

Some may say that there was no winner in regards to the War of 1812. Britain did not get her "naughty spaniel" back nor did the United States "liberate" British North America. To tell the truth, for Britain, the war had only really been a sideshow. When Napoleon returned to Paris on March 20, 1815, re-igniting the Napoleonic Wars, America and her little "Second War for Independence" was quickly forgotten. However, after the war, America and Canada would never be the same. It helped to define both countries shaping their identities and molding them into what they would become.

Canada did benefit from the war. It united them, not just the different areas such as Upper and Lower Canada, but the people became united as well. It helped both the English- and French-speaking races to develop a better understanding of each other as they fought a common enemy and it benefited British North America economically. Large sums of money flowed into the provinces. British pounds to shore up defenses and rebuild war-damaged towns and cities and American trade dollars flowed in during the British embargo. All of this would ultimately be a major factor in the unification of Canada in 1867. Arthur Lower, a Canadian historian, sums it up, "It therefore does not seem too far out to say that the War of 1812 is one of the massive foundation stones of modern Canada".

As for America, I do not think it could be better expressed than with the observation made by the French Minister Louis Serrier, "... the war has given the Americans what they so essentially lacked, a national character founded on a glory common to all." This "national character" would become most apparent 25 years later in the concept of Manifest Destiny, which would shape America and Americans for almost half a century. The war also gave the United States a new standing in the world community; they had stood up to and managed to withstand the most powerful military power of the time. The war also gave a renewed sense of national pride and purpose, "The war has renewed and reinstated the national feelings and character which the Revolution had given, and which were daily lessened. The people....are more American; they feel and act more as a nation; and I hope the permanency of the Union is thereby better secured." - Albert Gallatin, Secretary of the Treasury, 1816.

Besides the social effects, the war also affected the country economically, politically and militarily. American manufacturing capabilities increased during the embargo period, spurring on the production of everything from glassware to cotton goods. The high cost of the war also brought about the nation's first sales taxes on gold, silverware, jewelry, and watches. Politically, it spelled the end for the Federalist Party, their opposition to the war and their talk of secession had branded them as traitors and, in 1816, Rufus King had the dubious distinction of being the last Federalist candidate to run for president. The embarrassing defeats at the start of the war, as well as the burning of Washington, brought about significant military changes. There was increased emphasis on improving professionalism and training for U.S. Army officers and it brought about the movement to develop a standing army for defense versus relying upon state militias. Even though technically neither side won, the American sentiment was that they had prevailed. They felt unified as a nation, a nation that could face anything. The end of the war had brought in the new “Era of Good Feelings”.

An allegorical female figure of America leads pioneers and railroads westward, in accordance with the concept of Manifest Destiny. John Gast, 1872.

A TOWN'S STORY

A TOWN'S STORY:

Leading up to the War of 1812:

Prior to the American Revolutionary War, this area of upstate New York had been inhabited for thousands of years by differing cultures of indigenous peoples. The historic tribes were the Iroquoian-speaking Onondaga, part of the Haudenosaunee, or Iroquois Confederacy. Long trading with the French and English, most of the Six Nations allied with the British during the Revolution, hoping to dislodge the American colonists. Following the war, they were forced to make major cessions of most of their land in New York to the United States. Most of the Iroquois went to Canada and settled on land granted by Great Britain.

In the large-scale sales of 5 million acres (20,000 km^2) of public lands in the postwar period, Sackets Harbor was founded in 1801 by Augustus Sackett, a land speculator from New York City. He and others had high hopes for trade across Lake Ontario with Kingston and other parts of Canada. Sackets Harbor was the most significant community in the area until the founding of the City of Watertown. The area attracted migrants from New England, as well as immigrants from Great Britain and France. The latter were fleeing the turmoil of the French Revolution and the Napoleonic Wars. They cleared heavy forest and gradually constructed houses for a village center. Edmund Luff, a young English immigrant, constructed a non-denominational meetinghouse, where all Christians met until they built their own churches in later decades. By the 1810 census, there were 943 qualified voters in the village. After the War of 1812, Sackets Harbor incorporated as a village in 1814.

Northern view of Sacketts Harbor, N. Y.

The American Revolution did not resolve all issues with Great Britain. Border issues and increasing tensions led the US to impose the Embargo Act of 1807 prohibiting trade with Great Britain which effectively included Canada. People on both sides of the border, Canadian (many of them native Americans, including Loyalists who had fled there after the Revolution) and American, quickly built up a vigorous smuggling trade across the waters and through the nearby Thousand Islands area along the St. Lawrence River. The US government first stationed forces in the area to try to control smuggling.

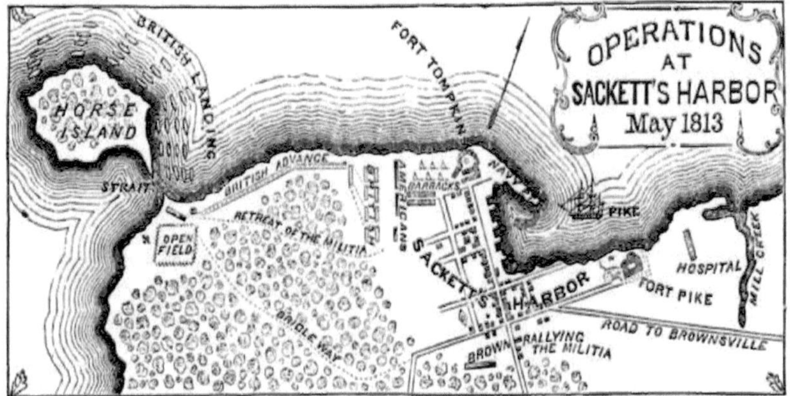

From Benton Lossing's "Pictorial Field-Book of the War of 1812" (pub. 1868)

The War Years:

As tensions increased with Great Britain, the US began to build up its military forces at Sackets Harbor, including creating a major shipyard at what became Navy Point. The scale of buildup was such that the citizens were outnumbered on a scale of about 8:1 by thousands of sailors and soldiers, camp followers and traders. Limited sanitary facilities and medical knowledge made dense troop encampments breeding grounds for infectious diseases such as typhus which quickly spread to villagers too.

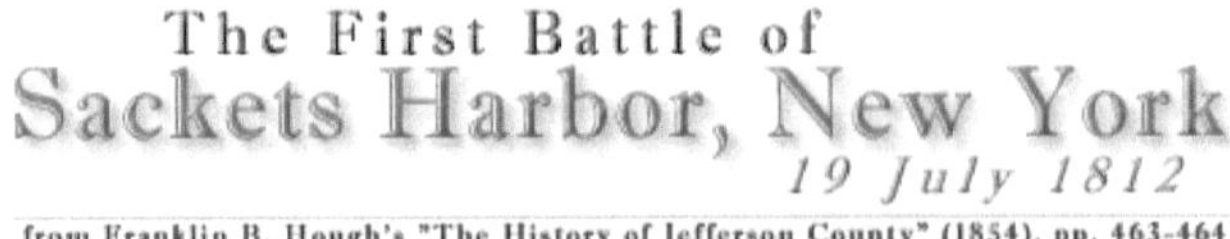

Commemorative postal cover issued by the Jefferson County Stamp Club in 1962. The picture is a reproduction of a mural owned by Flower Memorial Library in Watertown depicting the five ships that attacked Sackets Harbor in 1812, namely (from left to right): *Prince Regent*, *Royal George*, *Earl of Moira*, *Seneca*, and *Simcoe*.

The village was the site of two battles during the War of 1812. In the first battle in 1812, the brig USS Oneida and shore batteries repulsed an attacking force of five British ships. The village became a major base of operations for both the Navy (including US Marine Corps) and Army for the duration of the war. The Army built defensive earthworks around much of the village, and Fort Tompkins with barracks near Navy Point. Local militia built Fort Volunteer north of the village main streets. Thousands of troops gathered to defend the shipyard and village, and to attack Canada.

Battle of Sackets Harbor, Sunday, July 19, 1812:

On Sunday, the 19th of July, 1812, Captain Woolsey, of the Oneida, discovered from the mast head of his brig, five sails of the enemy beating up the harbor, including: the Royal George, 24 guns; the Seneca, 18; Prince Regent, 22; Earl of Moira, 20; and Simcoe. The Oneida attempted to gain the lake, but failing, returned, and was moored outside of the point, where the ship-house now is, with one broadside of nine guns to the enemy while the others were taken out and hastily placed on a breastwork on the shore, near which, on the day previous, a 32 pounder (intended for the Oneida, but found too heavy) had been mounted on a pivot upon a mound about six feet high. Alarm guns were fired, and expresses sent to call in the neighboring militia who did not, however, arrive in time to render assistance but who in the course of the day came in to the number of 3,000.

The British had, early in the morning, captured a boat laden with flour from Cape Vincent, and the crew were set on shore, and sent the message "that all they wanted was the brig Oneida, and the Lord Nelson (a vessel taken a little before for violation of the revenue), and that they would burn the village if there was a single shot fired at them."

The enemy had been misinformed about the defenses of the place, and especially of the 32 pounder, and supposed there was nothing to be feared in the way of ordinance. The force at that time in town was, besides the crew of the Oneida, the regiment of Colonel Bellinger, a volunteer company of artillery under Captain Camp, and a few militia.

Captain Woolsey, leaving his brig in charge of a lieutenant, took the general command on shore, the 32 pounder being in charge of Mr. William Vaughan, sailing master, and the other guns under that of Captain Camp. There were no shot in town larger than 24 pound balls which were used (with the aid of patches formed of carpet) in the 32 pounder.

By the time these arrangements were made, the enemy had arrived within gunshot range nearly in front of the battery when the action was begun, the first shot being from the 32 pounder on the mound, upon which a shout of laughter was heard from the fleet at the supposed imbecile attempt at resistance. The fire was returned briskly and continued for two hours all of the enemy's balls but one or two falling against the rocks at the foot of the bluff where our force was stationed. One ball fell nearby and plowed up the ground for some distance. It was caught up just as it had spent its force by a man who came running in and shouting that he had "caught them out," and so it proved for, from its commanding position, it was seen that our big gun had every advantage and that several of its shots told with effect.

Towards the close of the action, as the Royal George, the flag ship, was wearing to give another broadside, a 24-pound shot struck her stern and raked her whole length killing eight men and doing much damage. Upon this, the signal of retreat was given and the whole fleet bore away for Kingston without ceremony. At this, the band struck up the national tune of Yankee Doodle, and the troops, who had through the whole affair behaved like veterans, sent up three cheers of victory. The shots from our battery had broken their chest of medicines, their fore top gallant mast, and their vessels in a dozen places, while the enemy broke nothing but—the Sabbath.

In a letter to the governor of July 24th, General Brown attributed the success of the day to the gallant spirit of Woolsey, Bellinger and Camp, in their respective capacities, and especially to the nice shots of the 32 pounder. Mr. Vaughan, who had fired this piece, claims honor of having fired the first hostile gun in the war. One of the men at this gun, named Julius Torry better known as Black Julius, and a great favorite in the camp, served at his post with remarkable activity and courage. As there was no opportunity for the use of small arms, the greater part of the troops who were drawn up were spectators of the engagement.

The numbers of troops so exceeded what could be built to shelter them that in 1813 troops were housed with residents in stores, in barns and in tents. Village women counted themselves lucky if they were only cooking for officers. By the spring of 1813, the Army had gathered approximately 5,200 men in the village.

Most importantly, by 1813, the village became the US Naval Headquarters on the Great Lakes. Working at the Navy Point shipyard were 3,000 highly skilled men including hundreds of shipbuilders and carpenters brought from New York City because of a lack of locally skilled craftsmen. It was constructed and supervised during the war by New York City naval architect and shipbuilder Henry Eckford. They rapidly built eleven warships whose operations were critical to the United States' ability to defeat Great Britain for control of the Great Lakes.

The Second Battle of Sackets Harbor, May 1813:

In the second Battle of Sackets Harbor in May 1813, British forces landed and attacked the village but they were again driven off. Most of the American garrison and ships were at the opposite end of the lake at the time. The American defense was marred by officers' mistaken orders at Navy Point to destroy stores and a partially constructed ship to prevent capture by the British.

Until the federal government established the U.S. Naval Academy in Annapolis, Maryland, it had several schools for the training of midshipmen. Commodore Isaac Chauncey writing to the Secretary of the Navy on 30 November 1814 described a school established at Sackets Harbor on Lake Ontario in that year:

> *"Sir. I have the pleasure to inform you that I have established a Mathematical School under the direction of my Chaplain the Revd. Mr. Felch who is fully competent to the duties of such a School. More than One hundred Officers attend this School, as they can be spared from duty and about Sixty Lieutenants and Midshipmen attend daily who make great progress in the various branches of Mathematics Navigation."*
>
> *-Commodore Isaac Chauncey-*

Following the outbreak of war between the United States and Great Britain in June 1812, Sackets Harbor became the center of American naval and military activity for the upper St. Lawrence Valley and Lake Ontario. The brig Oneida with a company of marines was already at the harbor to suppress smuggling between northern New York and Canada. Local woodlands provided ample timber and a large fleet was constructed at the harbor's extensive shipyard. Barracks were also built for the thousands of soldiers, sailors, and mechanics who soon arrived to provide the manpower for the invasion and conquest of Canada.

To support the War of 1812, the US Navy built a major shipyard and its headquarters for the Great Lakes at the village. Within a short period, more than 3,000 men worked at the shipyard. The Army constructed earthworks, forts, barracks and supporting infrastructure to defend the village and navy shipyard and its troops also camped in town which was overwhelmed by the number of military.

In an attempt to destroy the American shipyard, a British-Canadian force launched an attack on May 29, 1813. At that time, the majority of the American forces were across Lake Ontario attacking Fort George. The remaining Americans drove off the enemy but their narrow victory was marred by a fire that destroyed their military stores. During the remainder of the war, Sackets Harbor was an active station where naval ships were constructed and supplied. In December 1814, the Treaty of Ghent officially ended the War of 1812 and the Lake Ontario fleet was placed in storage at Shiphouse Point.

The end of the war came in 1815 before the Navy completed construction of the last warship, the USS New Orleans. She was put into storage and never completed. She was scrapped in 1883.

An oil painting of the construction of naval ship, " New Orleans" being built in 1812-1815 in the Black River Bay. It was designed to carry a crew of 900 and never completed. It was ware-housed and then scrapped in 1883.

The Post-War Period:

Soon after the war, the Army strengthened its defenses on the northern frontier by constructing Madison Barracks. The village had a commercial shipyard and many business connections to communities around the Great Lakes. Its businessmen were also connected to bases in the major markets of Louisville, Kentucky and New Orleans. In 1817, a consortium of local businessmen supported construction of the 240-ton Ontario, the first US steamboat on the Great Lakes. In July 1834, the commercial schooner Illinois from Sackets Harbor was the first to enter the harbor of the new settlement of Chicago.

Additionally, the massive earthen fortifications protecting the harbor were graded off and the battlefield reverted to farmland. Several blockhouses were converted to barns and another became an office for the commandant of the Navy Yard.

The shipyard remained under Navy control because of the presence of an unfinished first-rate ship-of-the-line, the New Orleans. It was designed to carry a crew of 900 and was enclosed in a huge wooden ship house to protect it for future use. In 1817, the Rush-Bagot Agreement between the United States and Great Britain limited all naval forces on the Great Lakes. During the 1840s, old naval buildings were removed and new quarters were constructed for the naval commandant and sailing master (lieutenant) to meet the needs of a continuing naval presence.

The navy decided to scrap the New Orleans in 1883. The demolition of the vessel together with improved Canadian-American relations ended the need for a naval base in Sackets Harbor. The navy maintained the facility until 1955 although it was seldom used except for training by the state's naval militia.

Sackets Harbor Strategic Location:

The Village of Sackets Harbor, Jefferson County, New York is within the western part of the Town of Hounsfield and is west of Watertown. The heart of the village with a Main Street and well-preserved 19th century buildings has been recognized as the Sackets Harbor Village Historic District and listed on the National Register of Historic Places in 1983.

Because of its strategic protected harbor on Lake Ontario and the military installations built there, the village had national importance through the 19th century. To support the War of 1812, the US Navy built a major shipyard and its headquarters for the Great Lakes at the village. Within a short period, more than 3,000 men worked at the shipyard. The Army constructed earthworks, forts, barracks and supporting infrastructure to defend the village and navy shipyard, and its troops also camped in town which was overwhelmed by the number of military. Soon after the war, the Army strengthened its defenses on the northern frontier by constructing Madison Barracks. Sackets Harbor Battlefield State Historic Site commemorates a battle and the contribution of the area to the United States defense during the War of 1812.

The village had a commercial shipyard and many business connections to communities around the Great Lakes. Its businessmen were also connected to bases in the major markets of Louisville, Kentucky and New Orleans. In 1817, a consortium of local businessmen supported construction of the 240-ton Ontario, the first US steamboat on the Great Lakes. In July 1834, the commercial schooner Illinois from Sackets Harbor was the first to enter the harbor of the new settlement of Chicago.

The Battlefield Site Today:

The 1913 Centennial Park portion of the battlefield was recognized as early as 1866 as a special plot of land to be set aside to honor all the military personnel who had fought and died in the War of 1812. In 1878, the land was called the Old Battle Ground and was used for patriotic meetings, political rallies, church picnics, and other events. New York State took control of the Navy Yard in 1967 and began acquiring more of the historic battlegrounds including the most recent forty acres in 2006.

THE PEOPLE'S STORIES

Ignatius Cambron:

by: Kimberly Anne Cambern

In 1780, the same year that Lieutenant Colonel Banastre Tarleton slaughtered 113 Americans in the Waxhaw Massacre, Ignatius Cambron was born. The joy of his birth was overshadowed by the news of the bloodshed; as one witness described, "indiscriminate carnage never surpassed by the most ruthless atrocities of the most barbarous savages"; this was the setting that shaped young Ignatius' first years of life.

It is unknown which one of John Cambron's sons is Ignatius' father but it is without doubt that he is surely John's grandson. John and Susanna Cambron had four known sons: John Baptist, Leonard, James, and Thomas. Records show that John Baptist was more than likely too old to be Ignatius' father and Leonard died before Ignatius was born. Therefore, the most likely candidate would be either James or Thomas, with Thomas being the probable contender. However, no matter whether Ignatius' sire was James or Thomas, his father would have fought in the Revolutionary War, as all of John Cambron's surviving sons and two of his grandsons fought for independence.

Thomas Cambron and his wife Nancy lived in Charles County, Maryland where Thomas enlisted as a private in the 12th Battalion, Capt. Alexander McPherson's Company, 1777. Sometime right after the war, their family joined with the rest of Thomas' kinfolk and migrated to Kentucky. The Cambrons were all Roman Catholic and surely had raised their son Ignatius in the Catholic faith; in fact, most of the early immigrants to Kentucky were Catholic. The League of Catholic Families had been organized in 1785 to facilitate the migration to "The Holy Land of America" (Nelson County, KY); Ignatius would have been only 5 years old when he and his family left their home in Maryland for the Kentucky wilderness.

On November 18, 1806, Ignatius married Sarah (Sally) Beall, the daughter of Charles and Tabitha Beall. (Charles Beall was also a private in the Revolutionary War; 2nd Regiment, Frederick County, MD, Jan 1778 - Jan 10, 1780.). Ignatius and Sarah had five children: Henry Hamilton, James Bascom, Elizabeth, Sarah, and Amanda. However, these Cambron children would not be raised as Catholics for Sarah Beall was Presbyterian and, due to their marriage, Ignatius' family disowned him and never again acknowledged him or his children. Therefore, from that time forward, the descendants of Ignatius and Sarah would be raised as Presbyterians.

Shortly after the declaration of war against Britain, Territorial Governor General William Henry Harrison issued an address to the people of Kentucky calling for volunteers to defend the Indiana Territory. Thousands of Kentuckians answered the call including Ignatius. He enlisted as a private in Captain William Crouch's Company, 3rd Kentucky Mounted Volunteer Militia, commanded by Lieutenant Colonel James Allen. He commenced service on September 12, 1812 at Vincennes, Indiana Territory where, only eighteen days later, he is promoted to Corporal.

Fort Harrison, Indiana, 1812

By September of 1812, only Fort Harrison was left to protect the Indiana Territory. In July, Fort Mackinac had fallen to the British and, by August 14, the evacuation and massacre at Fort Dearborn with the subsequent surrender to the British had occurred. When the Pigeon Roost Massacre happened which occurred just days later, it became painfully obvious that it was imperative America hold Fort Harrison. So, early in October, after convalescing from a severe attack of fever and with a contingent of 4,000 Kentucky volunteers, half of which were mounted riflemen, General Samuel Hopkins headed north from Vincennes for Fort Harrison.

For more than two weeks, additional regulars, Indiana militiamen and more Kentucky volunteers poured into Fort Harrison, the final count may have been as many as 5 to 6,000 men. Finally, with more than sufficient troops to defend the fort, General Hopkins was ready to "clear out all Indian tribes" on the Wabash and Illinois Rivers and, on October 15, he set northward with 2,000 of his Kentucky mounted riflemen.

Only four days from Fort Harrison the trouble began, the men were still suffering from the fever that had swept through the troops, as well as rumors that the Indian scouts were disloyal and leading them astray was rampant. It was becoming increasingly evident that there was a lack of discipline and the men were getting more and more restless. Their complaints of lack of food, lack of equipment, lack of Indians to fight, as well as the inconvenience of having to put out numerous prairie fires believed to be set by the Indians, was making them "utterly mutinous". Therefore, on October 20, under the threat of revolt, a counsel of officers convened where the decision was made to return to Fort Harrison. Hopkins, in desperation to keep his expedition going, called for just 500 volunteers to continue on but there was not one response. The troops even refused to be commanded by him as they marched south, he was "forced to follow them".

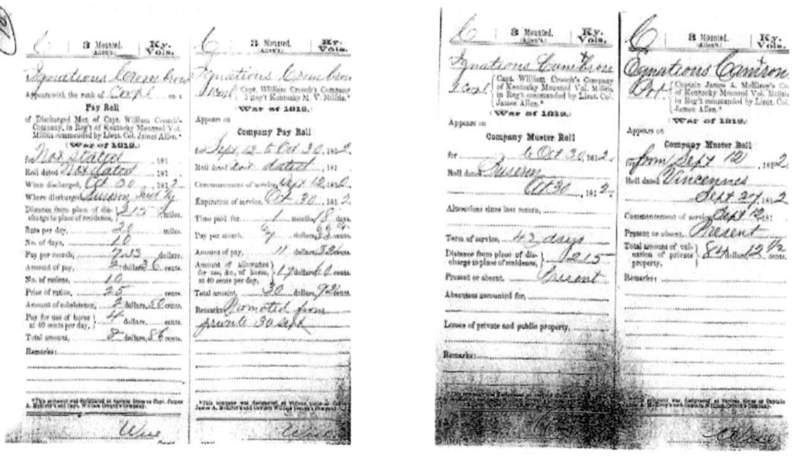
C | 3 Mounted (Allen's) | Ky. Vols.

Ignatious Cambron

Appears with the rank of Corpl on a

Pay Roll

of Discharged Men of Capt. William Crouch's Company, in Reg't of Kentucky Mounted Vol. Militia commanded by Lieut. Col. James Allen.*

(War of 1812.)

for Not stated, 181

Roll dated Not dated, 181

When discharged, Oct 30, 1812

Where discharged, Busseron, Ind Ty

Distance from place of discharge to place of residence, 215 miles.

Rate per day, 20 miles.

No. of days, 10

Pay per month, 7.33 dollars.

Amount of pay, 2 dollars, 36 cents.

No. of rations, 10

Price of ration, 25 cents.

Amount of subsistence, 2 dollars, 50 cents.

Pay for use of horse at 40 cents per day, 4 dollars, cents.

Total amount, 8 dollars, 86 cents.

Remarks:

C | 3 Mounted (Allen's) | Ky. Vols.

Ignatious Cambron

Corpl, Capt. William Crouch's Company, 3 Reg't Kentucky M. V. Militia.*

(War of 1812.)

Appears on

Company Pay Roll

for Sept 12 to Oct 30, 1812

Roll dated not dated, 181

Commencement of service, Sept 12, 1812

Expiration of service, Oct 30, 1812

Time paid for, 1 month, 18 days.

Pay per month, 7 dollars, 33 cents.

Amount of pay, 11 dollars, 73 cents.

Amount of allowance for use, &c., of horse, at 40 cents per day, 17 dollars, 60 cents.

Total amount, 30 dollars, 92 cents.

Remarks: Promoted from private 30 Sept

C | 3 Mounted (Allen's) | Ky. Vols.

Ignatious Cambron

1 Corpl, Capt. William Crouch's Company of Kentucky Mounted Vol. Militia, in Reg't commanded by Lieut. Col. James Allen.*

(War of 1812.)

Appears on

Company Muster Roll

for Oct 30, 1812

Roll dated Busseron, Oct 30, 1812

Alterations since last return,

Term of service, 43 days

Distance from place of discharge to place of residence, 215

Present or absent, Present

Absences accounted for,

Losses of private and public property,

Remarks:

C | 3 Mounted (Allen's) | Ky. Vols.

Ignatious Cambron

Pvt, Captain James A. McElroy's Co. of Kentucky Mounted Vol. Militia in Reg't commanded by Lieut. Col. James Allen.*

(War of 1812.)

Appears on

Company Muster Roll

from Sept 12, 1812

Roll dated Vincennes, Sept 27, 1812

Commencement of service, Sept 12, 181

Present or absent, Present

Total amount of valuation of private property, 84 dollars, 12 1/2 cents.

Remarks:

Pay stubs for Ignatious Cambron

On October 25, 1812, they are back at Fort Harrison without firing a shot or seeing an Indian. Five days later, General Hopkins discharges the mutinous mounted riflemen and sends them home.

There are no documents proving that Ignatius Cambron was a member of that ill-fated expedition but, as he was called for service on September 12, 1812 in Vincennes and discharged on October 30, 1812 in Buseron, Indiana Territory only serving 43 days, there is a good chance that he was. He never again served in the war and only 11 years later at the age of 43, he passed away at his home in Marion County, Kentucky.

AMOS CRITTENDEN, JR.:

by: Jennifer Doreen Schumann

My fifth Great Grandfather, Amos Crittenden, Jr., was born April 27, 1780 in Ashfield, Massachusetts. He was the first son of Amos Crittenden, Sr. and Phoebe McIntire. His father, Amos Crittenden, Sr., was a veteran of the Revolutionary War.

Amos Crittenden, Jr. grew up in Massachusetts, a region that was heavily dependent on importing and exporting goods to and from Europe. The War of 1812; also known as the Second Anglo-American War, was caused by America's desire to defend its rights as a neutral country to trade freely with other countries even if those countries were at war with Great Britain. Great Britain was engaged in trying to prevent America from trading with France during the war between Great Britain and France; which ultimately resulted in open warfare.

President Madison and the US Congress declared war with Great Britain despite the fact that the New England States; who had powerful economic interests, expressed strong opposition to the war. This war severely impacted trade between the U.S. and Europe during war times which caused economic hardship for the New England Region. As the war proceeded, the New England States began trading with its rivals along the Canadian boarder.

As the New England's elections ensued in the months ahead, some members of Congress who voted for the war did not get re-elected by the voters while others didn't seek re-election. The governors of Massachusetts, Connecticut, and Rhode Island refused to place their state militias under federal control for duty outside their particular states.

Opposition to the war extended beyond Federalist leaders as the US army of volunteers was on the decline. The New England States were rotating their volunteer soldiers in on a regular basis. Amos Crittenden, Jr. was enlisted as a Captain under the 4th

Regiment headed by Major General Ebenezer Mattoon. He was one of many soldiers that were engaged in the defense of Boston in autumn of 1814. His area of defense was the surrounding areas of Hampshire (which included Wendell, Warwick, Montague, New Salem, Shutesbury, Orange, and Northfield).

After he was discharged, he returned home to his wife, Mehetable Thomas, and their 4 children in Plainfield, Massachusetts.

Alexander Depew:

by: Catherine Brown

My fifth great uncle Alexander Depew fought in the War of 1812. My relation to him is through my paternal grandfather's side of the family.

Alexander Depew was born February 23, 1788 in Botetourt County, Virginia. He married Matilda Ward, the daughter of Captain James Ward, she was born on July 2, 1798 in Virginia. They were married on December 1, 1818.

Alexander's parents, Virginia natives, were Samuel Alexander Depew and Mary Rose Dean Depew. Samuel had fought in the Revolutionary War and after Samuel died, Mary married James Alexander and the whole family moved to Bourbon County, Kentucky in 1800.

During the War of 1812, Alexander R. Depew enlisted with the 16th Regiment (Porter's) Kentucky Militia. During the time that he served, he wrote a letter to a friend back in Paris, Kentucky about his time of service. He passed away in 1855.

PARIS, (Ky.) October 10.

A letter from Alexander R. Depew, esq., to a gentleman in this town, dated St. Mary's, October 1, 1812.

This day at twelve o'clock we arrived at this place, after a rapid journey of forty miles per day. We had heard on the road that Gen. Harrison was about to march to Detroit, and we wished if possible to join him before he set out. After we had passed Piqua about six miles, we met Capt. Trotter, of the Lexington dragoons, who informed us that Gen. Harrison would set out with all his army for Detroit in three weeks; that he had ordered Captain Garrard's troop of horse, from their march towards fort Defiance, back to this place to recruit their horses to fight the British in Canada; and that during those three weeks the mounted volunteers were to scour the frontier towards the head waters of the Wabash, and destroy all the Indian towns in that quarter. But an unexpected event, has for a time thwarted all these designs. A part of the army, composed of three regiments commanded by Cols. Allen, Scott, and Lewis also the regulars under Col. Wells, and Capt. Garrard's dragoons, all under the command of General Winchester, were on their march to fort Defiance, cutting their road as they went, and when they arrived within about four miles of the fort, they were surrounded by so large a body of Indians, that they were unable to proceed backwards or forwards. Yesterday about two o'clock P. M. an express arrived to General Harrison, from General Winchester, stating that the detachment under his command was entirely surrounded by a very large number of Indians; that they had been compelled to fortify their camp, by making a breast-work of logs on all sides of them. The breast-work is about five feet high. The express stated that in consequence of the Indians having surrounded them, they had received no provisions for several days; that they had nothing but beeves, and but few of them. And he desired immediate relief, lest his troops should be either starved to death or cut to pieces by the Indians. Two hours after the express came Gen. Harrison with his whole army marched to his relief. The express was brought by Thos. D. Carneal of Frankfort, and Abraham Ruddell. They say that from the trails of the Indians they must be equal to the army under Gen. Winchester (which is composed of two thousand men.) They further state that they saw the tracks of four or five wagons or carriages by which they suppose the Indians have cannon with them. They further state that five of the spies belonging to Allen's regiment were killed by the Indians and two wounded.

The army under General Harrison has advanced about twenty-five miles from this place. Capt. Trimble and myself shall set out tomorrow morning at daylight with five or six hundred mounted riflemen and infantry from the state of Ohio to join the army. We expect to have a battle the day after tomorrow, which will be the day on which we expect to reach fort Defiance.

N. B. Richard M. Johnson commands the regiment of mounted volunteers from Kentucky.

Ebeneezer Dodge:

by: Anita Speir

American Recruiting Song of the War of 1812

> Brave sons of the West, the blood in your veins
> At danger's approach waited not for persuaders;
> You rushed from your mountains, your hills, and your
> plains, and followed your streams to repel the invaders.

Standard Regulation Infantry Uniform: Uniform Coatee, white linen shirt, black neck stock, straight bottom trousers, half gaitors (Gaiters were worn over the bottom of the trousers to keep stones and dirt out of the shoes.), low quarter shoes, shako (The soldier's hat was the shako, a tall, cylindrical felt cap with an attached visor.), cartridge box with white buff sling, white buff baldric for bayonet scabbard, haversack, knapsack, tin canteen. The weapons used in the War of 1812 were knives, swords, bayonets, pistols, muskets, rifles, cannons and to a lesser extent, crude bombs. Among these different kinds of weapons, muskets, and rifles with bayonets were the most used and, in fact, were considered as the weapons that won the battles between these two opposing armies. This is because most battles were frontal in nature with wide distances between sides that would naturally call for the use of muskets and rifles. When it came to close combat fighting, the weapons used in the war of 1812 were bayonets attached on muskets and rifles; swords, knives were also used for close combat and pistols. However, pistols were usually used by army officers, thus, they were rarely used in close quarter fighting among soldiers.

The War of 1812 was not a popular war especially in New England, and the Governor of Connecticut Roger Griswold announced to President James Madison that his state's militia will not serve in the war against Britain. Massachusetts Governor Caleb Strong similarly refused to commit Massachusetts state

militia to the war effort on 5 August 1812. That was somewhat short-sighted and both states were involved in the war by 1813 due to the threat of invasion of New England by the British.

Twenty-nine years had passed since America's war with England for independence, and this was the second conflict for the same purpose. America had emerged from that Revolutionary War only a third-rate power, and England was never fully satisfied the war was over. England seemed ready to accept the first provocation for trouble and, if none was found, to furnish it herself. France and England were at war the greater part of the time.

The motivations of individual Enlisted Men were complex. Simple patriotism and stories of the Revolution must have played a role, as did the private's base pay of approximately $7.00 per month added to the initial $10.00 enlistment bounty and the $10.00 muster bounty, and the potential for a share in prize money from enemy ships and goods sold at auction through government agents; all of which no doubt appealed to underemployed unskilled young men seeking a steady income. United States recruiting speeches of the period emphasized: (1) Military glory, (2) Pay and bounties, and (3) A free suit of cloth (wool-rather than the farm boy's homespun linen) issued "not once but every year" of the five-year enlistment. Little to nothing is said of the politics or war.

The USA thought up a seemingly great idea: an embargo on American shipping might bring these countries to terms. But New England, being the most extensively engaged in shipping, was hardest hit. Nearly every seaport town in the United States sent up repeated protests and petitions to the Government for the repeal of the embargo, for they were all distressed by its workings. Secession from the Union was threatened.

Ebeneezer was from a Dodge family line that originated in England and went from Maine (then Massachusetts) USA to Halifax, Nova Scotia. Of course, with the shifting lines of ownership between the two countries, some of the time he was Canadian and some of the time he was American. At the time of the War of 1812, he was American and lived in Ashburnham, Worcester, Massachusetts. His Dodge line had been in Massachusetts for at least 100 years. He came from a family of 8 children and his mother's great grandfather, Richard More, came over on the Mayflower. The Dodges were pioneers, invested in this country and were here to stay.

Ebeneezer Dodge shows up in 1814 in Captain W. M. Reed's Company, Lieutenant Colonel E. Cutter's Regiment June 20 to June 28, June 24 to June 26, June 29 to July 5, and Sept. 10 to Sept. 28, 1814; service being at Boothbay, Maine.

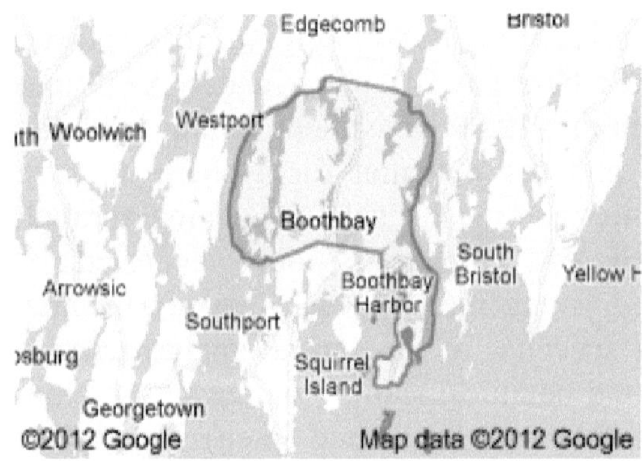

The first real action at Boothbay, after the declaration of war, June 18, 1812, was on the following July 7th. A special Safety Committee meeting sent a statement pleading to the President. They petitioned him "to grant them speedily the aid of a naval or land force as he may in his judgment think most proper and suitable to the situation, which will not only afford them that protection from the enemy which their present defenceless and unprotected state requires, but will also afford to the merchant and coasting vessels a most desirable place of security. And as in duty bound will over pray". The town treasurer was then directed to procure a sufficient quantity of bullet moulds.

General William King, Maine's first Governor, ordered out his entire division of militia, stationing most of his troops in Edgecomb. Meantime, nearly every man and boy, irrespective of age, who could handle a musket went into the local militia in Boothbay, Bristol and other neighboring towns.

It was thought best to try and raise a home force between Bristol and Boothbay. A Revolutionary war hero offered to do so and his services were gladly accepted. With forty-five men, they left Bristol and thirty Boothbay men joined the expedition. While laying in the harbor, they had sent to Wiscasset for some fieldpieces and more ammunition. They cruised about outside steadily for two days when, running short of provisions, went back into the harbor, returned the fieldpieces and ammunition, and the Boothbay contingent went to their homes.

On June 20, 1814, a 74-gun British ship entered the Sheepscot, landing six small boats somewhere on the west side of Boothbay, though opposed by about forty of the Boothbay militia. They marched between seven and eight miles but then met a larger force of Boothbay militia where they were beaten back, retreating to their boats and then to their vessel. June 27th and 28th other barges came into Boothbay Harbor but were fired upon from various points on the shore so that they left.

Though the darkest hour of the war along this part of the coast was in the latter part of 1814, at that very time the British cause was waning. A treaty was concluded December 24th that year and the news reached Maine sometime in February. Demonstrations of joy and victory then took place in nearly every town. The war had never been a popular one as had the struggle for independence through which the preceding generation fought but there was no lack of loyalty or patriotism in its support.

Thus ends the story of Ebeneezer Dodge in the War of 1812. Why are there not more Dodges from his family fighting in the war is unknown. Was he the black sheep? Was he ultra-patriotic? Did he just want a new pair of shoes and to get away from home? We will never know. But today, 200 years after the event, I am proud of Ebeneezer for leaving the comfort of home and fighting in an unpopular war to keep America free.

Samuel Folson, Jr.:

by: Marilyn L. Herst

Samuel Bradley Folsom, a distinguished Colonel in the Continental Army, was baptized in Exeter New Hampshire on June 28, 1747, and had a long service in the Revolutionary War. He first enlisted in Haverhill, Massachusetts in Captain Moses McFarland's Seventh Company, Lieutenant Colonel Thomas Nixon's Regiment before 1776. He subsequently served in several other regiments until he was discharged March 15, 1780.

Sackets Harbor Battle Banner 1812

Samuel Folsom Jr., one of Samuel B. Folsom's sons, and one of my great great great great great grandfathers was born March 2, 1784 in New Hampshire, then moved to upstate New York in the early 1800's to help settle the wild, untamed area known as Pillar Point in Jefferson County where Sackets Harbor is located. Samuel Folsom was an adventurer and seaman. He arrived in this area by sailing the St. Lawrence River, and settled in Brownville with his wife Rhoda who was born in New York near Sackets Harbor where he continued his love of the sea and building his life. According to an early map of the settled area, the Folsom family lived in Brownville on Pillar Point at the Black River Bay.

The Black River Bay was known as the finest and safest harbor on Lake Ontario with little wind and a deep water harbor; the town of Brownville at Pillar Point is located here. The Black River Bay is almost completely landlocked, surrounded by Trenton limestone edges that go up to thirty feet in height. This harbor covers an area of about sixty square miles with an abundance of water to float the heaviest ships. This is the location that the government chose to build the "New Orleans", a 72-gun frigate near the end of the War of 1812 with England.

In 1813, Samuel Folsom joined MCCLURE'S REGIMENT, NEW YORK VOLS. AND MILITIA to fight in the War of 1812 and defend the safety of his wife and his sons who lived in Brownville. Years later, Nelson and Ezra, two of his sons, carried on his tradition, becoming sailors on Lake Ontario, sailing steam ships and running a ferry boat business in the 1820's.

Map of New York State

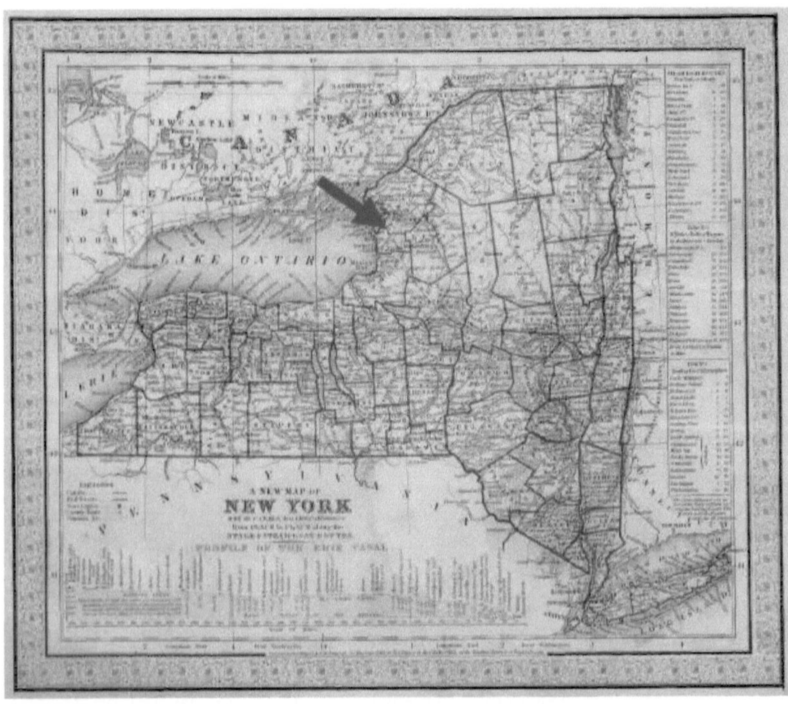

To get the full impact of understanding the enormous land and water mass in upstate New York, along with its close proximity to West Canada, this map gives an up close and personal view of the intricate tapestry of rivers, canals, lakes, forests, and the rural countryside of the early 1800's. Jefferson County is the focus of several of the battles with the British from 1812 to 1814. Due to the close proximity of Canada and the St. Lawrence River, this area became a likely area of conflict. The purple arrow is where Sackets Harbor, Jefferson County, NY is located.

Photo of Map of New York State: from the David Rumsey Collection.2005, Compiled from his large map of the state by David H. Burr, 1803-1875 Atlas of Maps, Rawdon, Clark & Co.

Map of Jefferson County

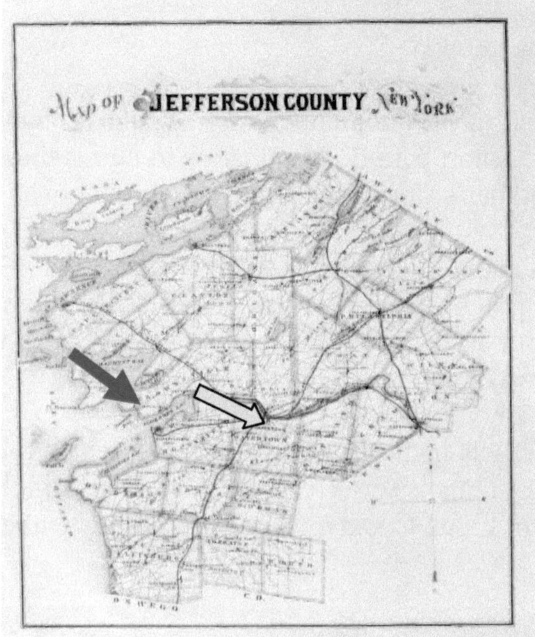

Jefferson County Map 1875

Brownville, located on Pillar Point is where the Battle of July 19, 1812 which is represented by the purple arrow. This is where the Folsom's and extended family made their home for over 200 years. They owned sawmills, and were sailors on the Black River and Lake Ontario.

Watertown is represented by the yellow arrow which became the hub of transportation and manufacturing in the middle 1800's, as the Black River flows through the middle of town creating a source of electricity

Alvin Francis:

by: Catherine Brown

My great, great, great, great grandfather Alvin Francis fought in the War of 1812 for a short period. My relation to him is through my paternal grandmother's side of the family.

Alvin Francis was a native New Yorker, born August 14, 1797 in Lewis Township, Essex County, New York. He married Elizabeth Soper (born July 22, 1797) October 1, 1818 who was also a native of New York.

Alvin and Betsey Francis had a family of nine children and their third child was Henry Francis (my great, great, great grandfather) who was also born in Essex County, New York on September 1, 1823.

Alvin and Betsey Francis

Alvin's parent (from Hamden, Massachusetts) were Samuel and Dorcas Francis. Samuel had fought in the Revolutionary War. The whole family moved to Erie County, Pennsylvania in 1832, were farmers there in Franklin Township, and in 1833, took up 134 acres of land.

Alvin Francis fought at the Battle of Plattsburg. After the war and farming, he was supervisor and Road Commissioner of Franklin Township in Essex County after moving there in 1832. The whole family were old-line Republicans, but were not active in their local government.

He was accidentally killed by falling off a scaffold in his barn in Erie County, Pennsylvania at 69 years old on February 9, 1867 and is buried in Girard Borough, Pennsylvania.

John Goss:

by: Teresa Summers née Goss

John Goss
Born 1795 of David and Elizabeth (Boss) Goss
Died 2 Apr 1849 (Age: 54)
Washington, Indiana, United States

My great-great-great grandfather John Goss was born in Rowan County, North Carolina, January 29, 1795. Arriving in 1727 at the Port of Philadelphia from Switzerland (see passenger list below), the Goss family hoped to obtain land there.

They did not remain in that area, however, and instead went to another of the original 13 colonies, North Carolina, where land was cheaper and easier to acquire. The first land record to a Goss is that granted for 480 acres to Frederick (Jr.) in Rowan County, North Carolina, on February 1st in the third year of the reign of George III (1763). Both Frederick Goss and his father-in-law Jacob Rickard were early planters and both men furnished supplies for the Continental Army during the Revolutionary War. Frederick Jr. also served in the local Rowan County regimental militia and was referred to as "Major" in the 1778 County tax list.

The family moved to Indiana around 1820. On August 18, 1825, John married Phoebe Crim in Indiana. She was the daughter of Martin born in Virginia in January 1780. (The senior Crims were members of Daniel Boone's party that came from Virginia to Kentucky).

John Goss was a farmer and public school teacher. His ciphering book, used as a text in teaching, still existed in the 1960's and carried the connotation, "John Goss his Ciphering Book in the year 1812." Both John and Phoebe are buried in the Meade Cemetery in Polk Township of Washington County, Indiana. Their children were all born in the same county.

John Goss's name appears on the muster rolls of the soldiers of the War of 1812 detached from the Militia of North Carolina in 1812 and 1814 (copy attached). Another relative, Joseph Goss Jr., is also shown in these rolls. He was a cousin of John.

Attachments: 1814 Muster Rolls, North Carolina

1778 Tax Rolls, Rowan County North Carolina

1727 Passenger List, ship *James Goodwill*

North Carolina - The War of 1812

1814 Muster - 6th Regiment - 2nd Company
Detached from the 2nd Rowan Regiment of NC Militia
Goss, John
Goss, Joseph Jr.

List of taxable property in the county of Rowan North Carolina, 1778

BURKHART, GEORGE	900	[illegible]
ROSS, PHILLIP	485	SP[illegible]
GOSS, FREDERICK-MAJ.	1035	HE[illegible]
GOSS, EPHRAIM	953	CO[illegible]
EIGLEBURGMAN, MARTIN	184	BL[illegible]

Passenger Ship's List of the *James Goodwill* for immigrants disembarking at Philadelphia

[List 2 A] A list of Palatyns, Imported In ye Ship James Goodwill, David Crockatt, Master, from Rotterdam, Sept 27, 1727

GASS, Frederich GASS, Jacob Jr. GASS, Jacob Sr.

Thomas Hall:

by: Sandra Warren

Thomas Hall was born November 1783 in Somerset County, New Jersey at the ending of the Revolutionary War. Along with his family and many others looking for desirable farming land, they migrated to the Northwest Territory where land had become available.

Bible record showing Thomas Hall's birth listed.

Frank C. Hall being first duly sworn says that he is of full age, is a resident of Lebanon, Warren County, Ohio, and that he has examined the Bible belonging to the family of John T. Hall; that the Bible appears to be quite old, and that the following record is contained in said Family Bible:

MARRIAGES

John T. Hall was married unto Hannah Lowe on the 13th day of February, 1783.

BIRTHS

John T. Hall was born on February 14th, 1763
Thomas Hall was born on Nov. 4th, 1783
Derrick Hall was born on Nov. 17th, 1785
Jacob Hall was born on Oct. 7th, 1787
Rebecca Hall was born on Oct. 25th, 1789
Mary Hall was born on July 21st, 1791
Ruth Hall was born on May 26th, 1793
Ann Wyckoff Hall was born on Oct. 19th, 1795
John Wyckoff Hall was born on Dec. 24th, 1797
Judah Lowe Hall was born on Oct. 19th, 1799
Nella Hall was born on September 26th, 1802
Cornelius Lowe Hall was born on July 16th, 1804
Julia Phillips Hall was born on Nov. 17th, 1807

The land tax records show Thomas Hall owned and paid taxes on land in Deerfield Township, Warren County, Ohio in the year of 1810. He had purchased the land in 1809 for the sum of one thousand dollars.

By 1811, Thomas Hall and Sarah Ann Wikoff had married on September 10. Aat that time, Thomas was 28, and Sarah was 15 years old. They set up housekeeping on a farm in the northeast part of the township near the Little Miami River and their family would grow to 13 children. Sarah Ann's father, Peter Wikoff, issued his consent.

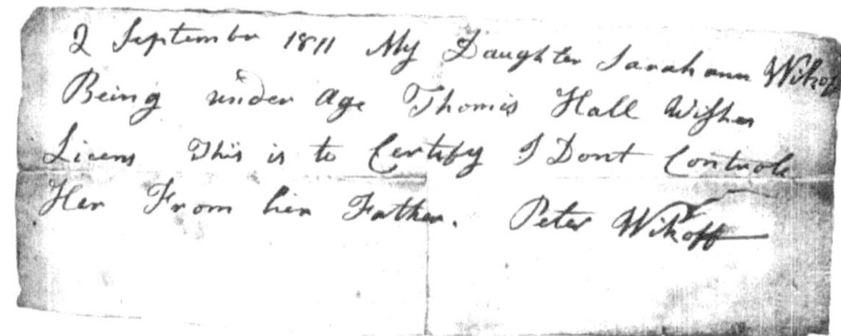
2 September 1811 My Daughter Sarah ann Wikoff Being under age Thomas Hall Wishes Licens This is to Certify I Dont Controle Her From her Father. Peter Wikoff

The Roll of field and staff for the War of 1812-1813 shows Thomas Hall serving with Colonel James Findlay, Second Regiment, Ohio Militia as a Private.

War of 1812 Service Records

Name:	**Thomas Hall**
Company:	2 REGIMENT (FINDLAY'S), OHIO VOLS. AND MILITIA.
Rank - Induction:	PRIVATE
Rank - Discharge:	PRIVATE
Roll Box:	89
Roll Exct:	602

Source Information:
Direct Data Capture, comp.. *War of 1812 Service Records* [database on-line]. Provo, UT, USA: Ancestry.com Operations Inc, 1999. Original data: National Archives and Records Administration. *Index to the Compiled Military Service Records for the Volunteer Soldiers Who Served During the War of 1812*. Washington, D.C.: National Archives and Records Administration. M602, 234 rolls.

Description:
This database is a listing of men mustered into the American armed forces between 1812 and 1815 for the War of 1812. Taken from records in the National Archives, each record includes the soldier's name, company, rank at time of induction, rank at time of discharge, and other helpful information. It provides the names of nearly 600,000 men.

Returning from the war, Thomas and family continued to farm increasing their land holdings with their family growing. They took part in community efforts to build a meeting house to be open and free for any society whatever. In the year of 1817, the building was used by the Baptists who organized a society there.

Thomas lived until 1862, his life spanning 79 years. After Sarah was widowed, she continued to live on the farm with her son Peter and there she died at 95 years of age. She had 72 grandchildren, 158 great grandchildren and 13 great great grandchildren at the time of her death.

Thomas Hall; buried at the Fellowship Church Cemetery. On Sunday mornings, when the sound of church hymns mingled with the song of the birds, it is the perfect resting place for the many buried in the cemetery surrounding the "Little White Church by the Side of the Road" *(by Jessie Van Meter)*.

John Harbison:

by: Anita Speir

The War of 1812 rolled its drums in Pennsylvania when war was declared against Britain. Volunteers were called to defend the Canadian border and the pioneers of Butler County responded with a regiment of twelve companies under the command of Colonel John Purviance. John Harbison Jr., eldest living son of John William Harbison Sr., and the 2nd great grand uncle of Anita Speir, enlisted for the campaign as a private in the Third Company under Captain James Thompson.

In 1792, John's mother, Massey White Harbison, and her first three children were captured by the Indians and held in captivity. Two of the children were killed by the Indians but Massey managed to escape with her infant and make her way back to civilization. That infant was John Jr.

Many of the sturdy men who became the pioneers of Butler County were soldiers of the Revolutionary War, who after its end, took up the work of clearing the forest and establishing homes for themselves and their families on what was then the western frontier. When the encroachments of Great Britain made a second war necessary, these veterans were among the first to offer their services in defense of their flag and country, inspiring those of the younger generation to a quick response to the call to arms.

On July 19, 1812, the appearance of the British fleet off Presque Isle, Maine, indicated determination on the part of the enemy to not only destroy the half-finished American fleet but to invade the State itself.

Citizens to Arms

Your State is invaded. The enemy has arrived at Erie, threatening to destroy our navy and the town. His course, hitherto marked with rapine and fire wherever he touched our shore, must be arrested. The cries of infants and women, of the aged and infirm, the devoted victims of the enemy and his savage allies, call on you for defense and protection. Your home, your property, your all require you to march immediately to the course of action. Arms and ammunition will be furnished to those who have none at the place of rendezvous near to Erie, and every exertion will be made for your subsistence and accommodations. Your service to be useful must be rendered immediately. The delay of an hour may be fatal to your country, in securing the enemy in his plunder and favoring his escape.

David MEAD, *Maj. Gen. 19th D. P. M.*

One of the ways of enlisting men for the regular army was by placing and rattling silver coins on a drumhead which were free to all who were capable of being mustered into the service and whoever took one of them off was held to be enlisted.

After being fully recruited, the volunteer company was moved, along with other companies, from the Allegheny Mountains to Meadville, Pennsylvania, in September, 1812 where it was assigned to the 1st Infantry Regiment of the Pennsylvania detachment commanded by Col. Jeremiah Snyder. It and the 2nd Regiment Infantry commanded by Colonel John Purviance of Butler, Pennsylvania, the 1st Regiment of Riflemen commanded by Colonel Jared Irwin, and the 2nd Regiment of Riflemen commanded by Colonel William Piper, were brigaded at Meadville.

The volunteer troops were held at Meadville until the end of October and Colonel Purviance's regiment until about the 1st of November because their firearms were defective. When properly inspected, one half of them were found to be totally unfit for service. So that instead of marching immediately to the place of destination as General Tannehill had expected, he was under the embarrassing position of sending teams to Pittsburgh for a supply to make up the deficiency. Between two and three weeks, therefore, were lost. It is said that the deficiency of proper arms was caused by the shameful decisions of brigade inspectors. Furthermore, the amount of money was sufficient to pay off only three regiments so that seven or eight days were lost in a trip to Pittsburgh to obtain enough to pay off the fourth regiment.

A considerable number of that detachment of Pennsylvania volunteers, while at Meadville, PA expressed their determination not to cross over into Canada. Some of those volunteers must have either lost their courage or become weary of military service before their brigade moved to that rendezvous. The Sunbury Times, PA, dated October 9 said that a volunteer from a neighboring county had deserted and returned home, and that "his wife refused speaking to him or having anything to do with him unless he would return." So he shouldered his knapsack and retraced his steps to Meadville. The same paper also complained about the arrival at (the town of) Sunbury of five deserters from Captain Jared Irwin's rifle company which had been recruited in that same part of Northumberland County. They were promptly arrested and confined in jail if they did not consent to return to their corps.

But John Harbison Jr. did fight in the war making his father, John Harbison Sr. (famous Indian Spy and Revolutionary War veteran) proud in the fight to keep America free from British infiltration. When it was over, John Jr. returned, married and lived for a time on Bull Creek in Pennsylvania. He was then lured by the tales from the west and followed the stream of emigrants with his eleven children into the Mississippi Valley. He and the other veterans of this war proved that the Americans were here to stay.

The following is information about his gravesite in Ohio.

U.S. Veterans Gravesites, ca.1775-2006

Name:	John Harbison
Service Info.:	PVT US ARMY WAR OF 1812
Birth Date:	6 Mar 1784
Death Date:	27 Oct 1857
Cemetery:	Pioneer Cem #81
Cemetery Address:	3868 Church St Greenville, OH 45331

John Leonard:

by: Sandra Warren

1782 – 1824; My grandmother's great, great grandfather John Leonard served in the War of 1812 against Great Britain.

John Leonard was born in 1782 near the ending of the Revolutionary War. His father Joshua had served in the Revolutionary War for the New Jersey Militia for freedom from Britain's hold. At family gatherings, the stories of the war efforts were shared and passed down by word of mouth. John learned of Vermont where his father had been stationed near Lake Champlain; heard about the rich and fertile lands and potential mill sites on innumerable streams and rivers and of the military roads already established for access.

In 1803 when John married Catherine Kitchell, they removed to the township of Addison, Addison County, Vermont. They had a good start with John trained in the family trade of iron works, making everything from kitchen tools to plows and axes and much more. Catherine was fully trained in home economics taught by her mother, with both being experienced in farming all their lives. There they farmed successfully and four of their seven children were born.

With the strains between Great Britain and the United States, the Lake Champlain area was greatly affected financially regarding the shipping and exporting of their goods. Not far from Addison, populations increased with the emergence of the Monkton Iron Works which grew to employ hundreds. Vermont's iron-making industry developed in association with other pioneer works such as grist and saw mills, blacksmith shops in response to the needs of early settlers.

The success of the Monkton Iron Works generally coincided with the War of 1812, as the U. S. Navy placed an order with the company to deliver 300 tons of cannon shot.

The city was placed on the map militarily as the United States Navy placed the fleet's winter quarters near to the location of the iron works. The strains imposed upon shipping of their goods was about to effect the economic base throughout the area.

For John and Catherine, their life in Vermont had been busy times with the four children to care for, as well as farming and everyday concerns. In 1805, there was a severe drought on the west side of the Green Mountains, followed in 1811 by floods. Then the grasshoppers' attack of 1812 devastated all the crops in their path.

With the approach of the War of 1812, John and Catherine decided to move their family to Ohio State. They traveled from Vermont by wagon team across New York and Pennsylvania to Pittsburg. From there, by flatboat down the Ohio River to Cincinnati then 22 miles to the present site of Mason, Warren County, Ohio to establish their new home. Both John and Catherine had extended family already located in the Mason, Ohio area.

The family settled into their new home, started farming and John enlisted in the Army. He enlisted as a private in Captain Ferguson's Company, Second Regiment of the Ohio Volunteers. The terms of duty were for twelve months for the Ohio Volunteers but it was not indicated if these were consecutive months or broken months. While John was away, Catherine and her young family ran the family farm with help from extended family.

After the war John worked at increasing their land holdings and their family continued to increase too. Ohio was becoming a breadbasket state with prime land to yield good crop production. Along with this, the shipping of the agricultural goods was improving with the canals across Ohio and the railroad routes. Profits were increasing with this rapid commercial expansion.

Then John's untimely death in 1825 was the source of deepest sorrow for Catherine, left with seven children, the youngest a babe of six months. The family continued to support themselves with the farm John had built up. John had taught them the necessary skills to take each family member forward in their lives. And he taught them to play music for entertainment. He was buried on the farm on the family grounds and later re-interred at Rose Hill Cemetery in Mason, Ohio.

Attachments:

1. Army enlistment.
2. Map showing fronts on which the land war of 1812 was fought
3. Land Warrant issued to his heirs;
4. Township map showing location of the land;
5. Letter showing placement of grave on farm.
6. Photo of some of John's descendents. (seated: John Leonard jr.-son; Amily Leonard McCowan – daughter; Donnah Maria Leonard Mewhinney – daughter. Other's are grandchildren and great grand children to John Leonard)
7. Newspaper clipping War of 1812.

Page 1 of 1 Page 1 o

ancestry.com

U.S. Army, Register of Enlistments, 1798-1914

Name: **John Leonard**

Birthyear: abt 1783

Enlistment Age: 30

Source Information:

Ancestry.com. *U.S. Army, Register of Enlistments, 1798-1914* [database on-line]. Provo, UT, USA: Ancestry.com Operations Inc, 2007.

Original data: Register of Enlistments in the U.S. Army, 1798-1914; (National Archives Microfilm Publication M233, 81 rolls); Records of the Adjutant General's Office, 1780's-1917, Record Group 94; National Archives, Washington, D.C.

Description:
This database contains a register of enlistments in the U.S. Army from 1798-1914. Information listed on these records includes name of enlistee, age at time of enlistment, birthplace, and date of enlistment.

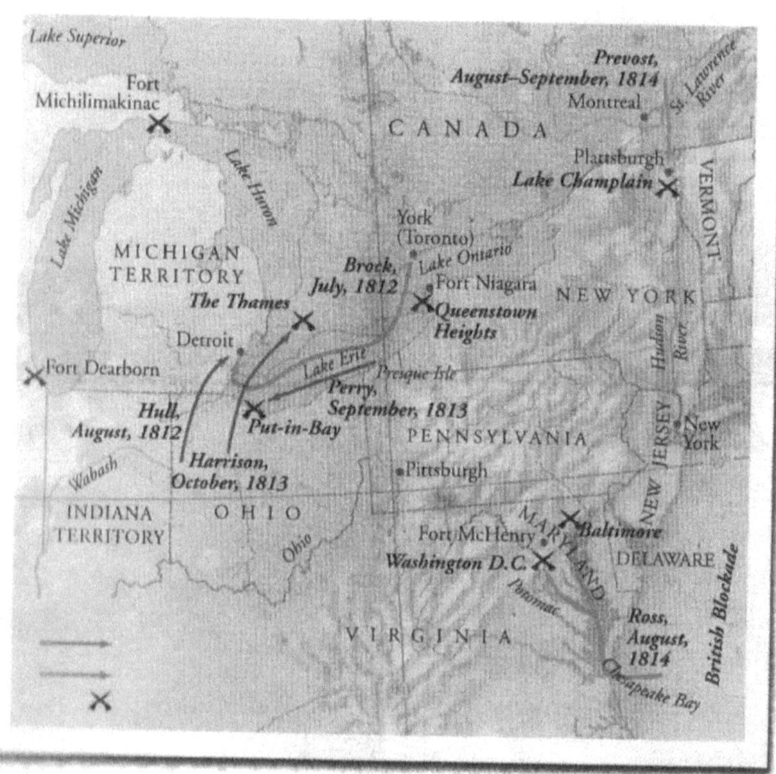

The map shows the many fronts on which the land war of 1812 was fought. While the U. S. Army sought to attack Canada and control the Great Lakes, the British Navy sacked Washington and shot up Fort McHenry in Baltimore, Maryland.

UNITED STATES OF AMERICA,

To all to whom these Presents shall come, Greeting:

Whereas, Warrant No. 84570 for 160 acres, issued under authority of the act of Congress approved the 11th day of February 1847 entitled "An Act to raise for a limited time an additional Military force and for other purposes, in the name of John Leonard, late a Private in Captain Ferguson's Company Second Regiment Ohio Volunteers

has been returned to the GENERAL LAND OFFICE, with evidence that the same has been located in pursuance of said act, and the Act approved August 14, 1848 entitled an Act in relation to Military Land Warrants, by the said John Leonard on the South West quarter of the North West quarter and the North West quarter of the South West quarter of Section Thirty six in Township Five North, of Range Four East in the District of Lands subject to sale at Defiance Ohio, containing Eighty Acres according to the Official Plat of the Survey of the said Land returned to the *GENERAL LAND OFFICE*, by the SURVEYOR GENERAL; and, whereas, said location heretofore suspended, has been confirmed to said locator under the provisions of the act of Congress approved 3d March, 1853, entitled "An Act to revive and continue in force for a limited time the provisions of an act relative to suspended entries of public land."

Now Know Ye, That there is granted by the UNITED STATES unto said John Leonard

the tracts of Land above described; TO HAVE AND TO HOLD the said tracts of Land, with the appurtenances thereof unto the said John Leonard and to his

heirs and assigns forever.

In testimony whereof, I, Franklin Pierce

PRESIDENT OF THE UNITED STATES OF AMERICA, have caused these Letters to be made Patent, and the SEAL OF THE GENERAL LAND OFFICE to be hereunto affixed.

GIVEN under my hand, at the CITY OF WASHINGTON, the Tenth day of July in the year of our Lord one thousand eight hundred and Fifty Four and of the INDEPENDENCE OF THE UNITED STATES the seventy-Ninth

27360

{SEAL.}

BY THE PRESIDENT: Franklin Pierce

By A E Baldwin asst Sec'y.

J. N. Granger Recorder of the General Land Office.

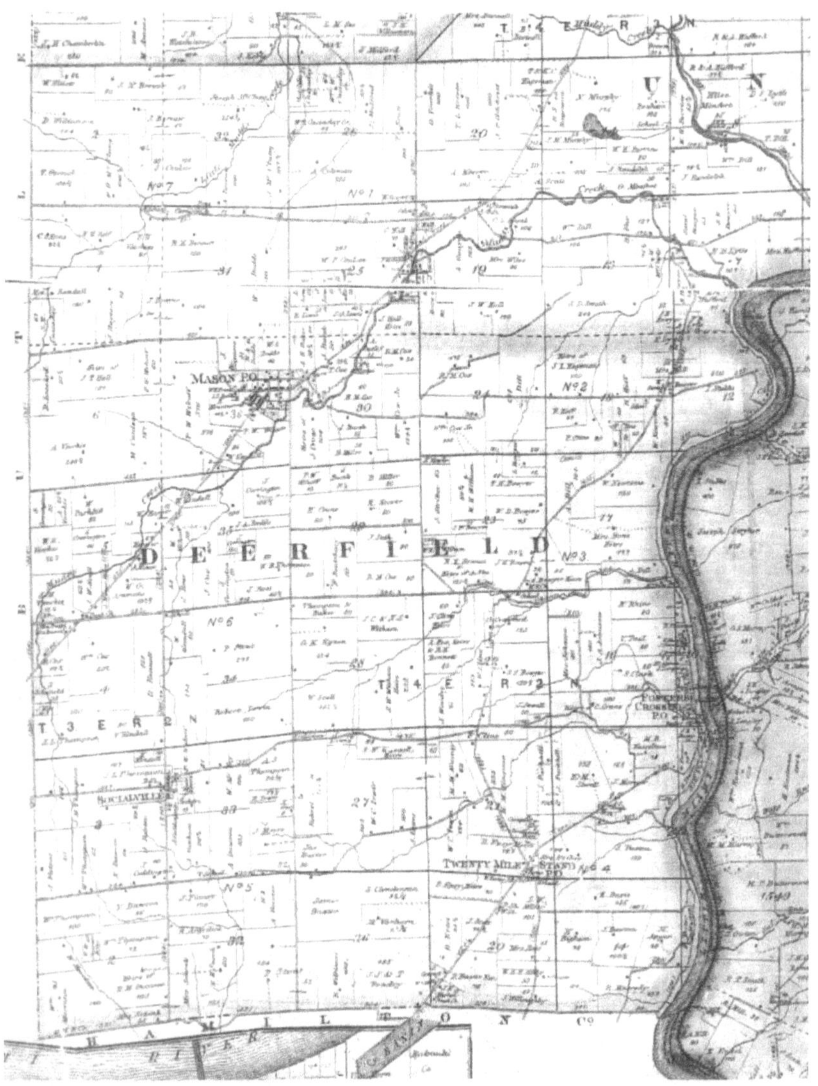
D E E R F I E L D
MASON P.O.
SOCIALVILLE
TWENTY MILE STAND P.O.
No 2
No 3
No 4
No 5
No 6
No 7
H A M I L T O N Co

Ukiah Cal. Nov. 23" 1934

Dear Cousin

Yours of Sept. 12" has remained unanswered for serial reasons, principally weak eyes and some business entanglements.

Many years ago brother George visited in Mason, and one of Uncle Alex sons showed him over the old farm, pointing out the last resting place of Grand Father Leonard. On his return George told me that the grave was encroached on by a rail fence.

There many years ago my mother told me of the passing of Grand Father Leonard, the subject was never mentioned in my presents again, and there was no doubt in her mind regarding it.

I wonder where May Totten got the information that Hal Jr. was going to publish a book on family history.

Back Row - John Mawhinney - Dr. George McCowen - Mary E. (Pimpkin) McCowen - May Carpenter - Blanche (McCowen) Landis -
Bonnie (") Brunner.
Seated - John Leonard Jr. - Thomas McCowen - Emily (Leonard) McCowen - Hannah Maria (Leonard) Mawhinney -
Helen (") Carpenter - Emily (") Horton.
Children - Frank Carpenter - born - 11 - 8 - 1870.
Arthur Horton - " - 8 - 4 - 1873.

THE WASHINGTONIAN.

Vol. III.] WINDSOR, (VERMONT) MONDAY, AUGUST 17, 1812. No 109

ADDRESS

OF

Members of the House of Representatives,

OF THE CONGRESS OF THE UNITED STATES,

TO THEIR CONSTITUENTS,

ON THE SUBJECT OF THE

WAR WITH GREAT BRITAIN.

(Concluded from our last.)

So familiar to them was the existence of the decrees, and such their eagerness to give them effect against our commerce, that they feigned a violation to have taken place, and that notwithstanding the express give them effect against our commerce, that they feigned victim declaration of the captain and crew, to the contrary. In addition to which evidence, Mr. Russell's letter to the Secretary of State, dated 9th May 18 , says "it may not be improper to remark that "no American vessel captured " since the 1st Nov. 1810 has yet been released."

From this it is apparent, that the commanders of the national vessels, the privateersmen, and the judges of the prize courts, to which may be added also the custom house officers, who, as the instruments of carrying into effect the decrees, must have been made acquainted with the repeal had it existed, have been from first to last, ignorant of any revocation ; and uniformly acted upon the principle of their existence.

Etienne Lucier:

by: Teresa Summers née Goss.

09 Jun 1786, Boucherville, QC - 08 Mar 1853, St Paul, Marion Co., OR

My fourth great-grandfather, Etienne Lucier, did not directly participate with the Patriots in the War of 1812 for one primary reason: he was living thousands of miles away at the first American settlement west of the Rocky Mountains, Fort Astoria, in what is now Oregon.

In 1811 American fur-trader and entrepreneur John Jacob Astor sent two exploratory parties to the mouth of the Columbia River, to start a trading company with all its attendant outposts. One party traveled by land, the other by sea on the Ship *Tonquin.*

Upon arrival of the *Tonquin* in 1811, officers and employees of Astor's Pacific Fur Company, controlled by Americans, started building its primary fur trading post in the Northwest. With the foundation of Fort Astoria in 1811, the Canadian North West Company had a competitor on the Pacific Coast and northern interior.

My great-great-great-great grandfather was part of the overland party led by the American Wilson Price Hunt. They arrived at Fort Astoria in February 1812, after a long and arduous trip. (See Hunt's diary, *Voyage of Mr. Hunt and his companions from St Louis to the mouth of the Columbia by a new route across the Rocky Mountains).*

During the War of 1812, the Montreal-based North West Company pressured the Royal Navy to capture the base of their rival, Astor's Pacific Fur Company. On March 25, 1813, the British dispatched two ships from England, the *Isaac Todd* and the *Phoebe*, under secret orders to destroy any American settlement on the Columbia River or the Pacific Coast. The ships

Raccoon and *Cherub* joined them during the voyage as the slow-sailing Todd slipped farther and farther behind. The *Raccoon* [aka *Racoon*] was sent ahead to the Northwest as the other British warships battled and defeated the American ship Essex off the coast of Valparaiso, Chile.

Before the *Racoon* arrived at their proposed destination of the fur trading outpost of Fort Astoria, however, the North West Company had completed a deal with the Pacific Fur Company that since British ships would be imminently arriving to "take and destroy everything American on the Northwest coast," they would purchase the assets, for a third of their value. Captain William Black. Even though Captain William Black arrived to find the matter already settled, could not resist the temptation of “taking” the fort, thus conducting a ritual of hauling down the American flag and running up the British in its place. Captain Black renamed it Fort George. Black claimed possession of the Columbia River drainage for Great Britain on December 13, 1813. The *Raccoon* sailed way from Ft. Astoria on New Year’s Day, 1814. Later Black reported to the Admiralty, referring to the Astorians as the "Enemy party," that they were "quite broken; they have no settlement whatever on this river or coast."

In 1818, only on an extraordinary interpretation of the Treaty of Ghent, Fort Astoria was restored to America. The diplomatic restoration was verbal, and for the fort only, not the country. Later, the Americans claimed the restoration of the country, and there was no legal paper or documentary proof of the fact that only the fort had been restored. As a matter of fact, the treaty provided for the return of forts captured during the war; Astoria was bought and paid for, even though it was through fear of capture.

Etienne Lucier was directly affected by these changes and, as an original “Astorian,” no doubt was in the vicinity when the British took over the fort.

In 1821 the North West Company was merged into the Hudson's Bay Co., which took ownership of the fort. Lucier shows as an employee in Hudson's Bay Company archival records.

Lucier stayed in Oregon country the rest of his life. He married a native woman, Josephte Nouite, who was, according to Oregon Census records, born in Oregon Territory. He participated in contacting the Roman Catholic Bishop of Montreal requesting that a Catholic priest be sent to the region, known as "French Prairie" due to all the French settlers. Etienne and Josephte were "legally" married by such a priest on January 23, 1839 at the nearby British-run Fort Vancouver, just a year before she died.

In 1843, Lucier was one of only two French Canadians who cast the pivotal deciding votes to establish an American-style Provisional Government in Oregon. Eligible voters included 102 farmers, trappers, laborers, and adventures who gathered that day including 52 who came from Canada and 50 who had come to Oregon from American states. Fifty Americans voted for "an American divide" [from Canada and Great Britain]. Before official vote count, Francis X. Matthieu (a Canadian opposed to British ways) joined the group, accompanied by his friend Etienne Lucier, also a Canadian. A vote of 52-50 settled the issue. In 1851 Lucier became an American citizen in order to secure his land claim via the Donation Land Act.

The Fort Astoria Site was added to the list of National Historic Landmarks on November 5, 1961. It is marked by a reconstructed block house in Astoria.

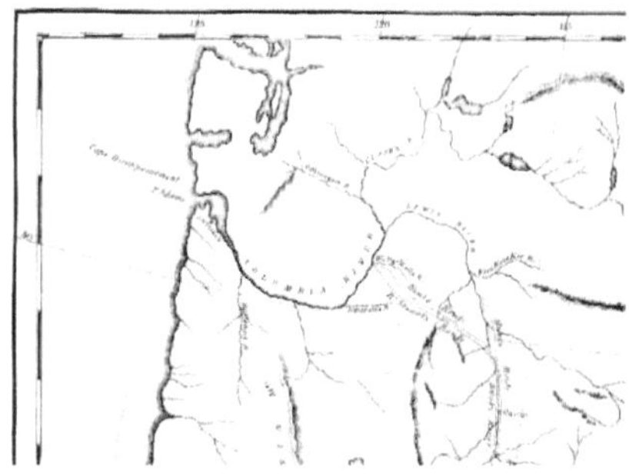

Hunt Expedition Map 1811-1812

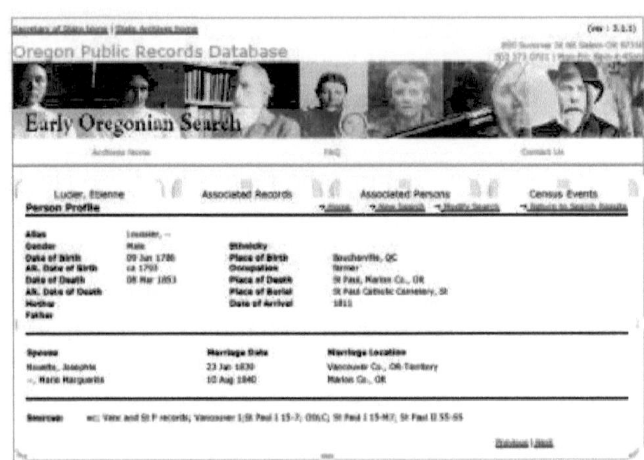

Oregon Public Records Database

Early Oregonian Search

Lucier, Etienne | Associated Records | Associated Persons | Census Events

Person Profile

Alias	Loussier, --		
Gender	Male	**Ethnicity**	
Date of Birth	09 Jun 1786	**Place of Birth**	Boucherville, QC
Alt. Date of Birth	ca 1793	**Occupation**	farmer
Date of Death	08 Mar 1853	**Place of Death**	St Paul, Marion Co., OR
Alt. Date of Death		**Place of Burial**	St Paul Catholic Cemetery, St
Mother		**Date of Arrival**	1811
Father			

Spouse	**Marriage Date**	**Marriage Location**
Nouette, Josephte	23 Jan 1830	Vancouver Co., OR-Territory
--, Marie Marguerite	10 Aug 1840	Marion Co., OR

Sources: wc; Vanc and St P records; Vancouver 1;St Paul I 15-7; OD(C); St Paul I 15-M7; St Paul II 55-65

Previous | Next

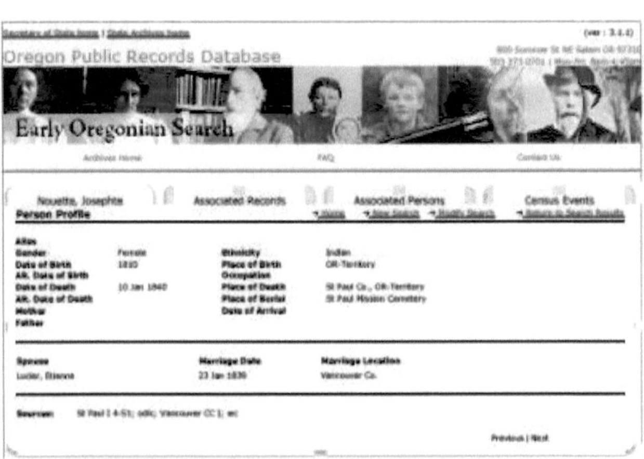

Oregon Public Records Database

Early Oregonian Search

Nouette, Josephte | Associated Records | Associated Persons | Census Events

Person Profile

Alias			
Gender	Female	**Ethnicity**	Indian
Date of Birth	1810	**Place of Birth**	OR-Territory
Alt. Date of Birth		**Occupation**	
Date of Death	10 Jan 1840	**Place of Death**	St Paul Co., OR-Territory
Alt. Date of Death		**Place of Burial**	St Paul Mission Cemetery
Mother		**Date of Arrival**	
Father			

Spouse	**Marriage Date**	**Marriage Location**
Lucier, Etienne	23 Jan 1830	Vancouver Co.

Sources: St Paul I 4-51; odc; Vancouver CC 1; wc

Previous | Next

On the 19th ult., at his house on his claim in the vicinity of Champoeg, Marion County, Oregon Territory, ETIENNE LUCIERE, about 65 years of age, born in the parish of Acadea, Lower Canada. He came to this country in 1812 as one of the late J. J. Astor's engaged servants, with Messrs. Hunt and McKenzie, the leaders of the party, and remained in the country ever since, till 1829, as a trapper;—that year he took a claim opposite to Portland: in 1830 he abandoned it. In 1831 he took the claim on which he ended his days.—He is the first white man that settled on a claim in Oregon Territory. He was an excellent neighbor, an industrious, honest man, which, joined together, make a good citizen and a valuable member of society.

Lucier Grave Marker, St. Paul, Oregon

Willamette Settlers to the Bishop of Juliopolis

Catalog Number: Mss 83
Date: 1836

Address of Willamette Settlers Transcription
(**This transcription has been edited for spelling and punctuation**)

Willamette March 22th, 1836
To the Bishop of Juliopolis

Reverend sir

We received your kind letter last fall, which gave us much pleasure and ease to our minds for it has been a long time since we have heard the likes of it. It gave us a new heart since we received your kind instructions to us. We will do our best endeavors to instruct our families to your wishes, still living in hopes to some speedy relief which we are looking for with eager hearts for the day to come. Since we received your kind letter we have begun to build and make some preparations to receive our kind father, which we hope will not be in vain for you know our situation better than ourselves for some of us stand in great need of your assistance as quick as possible. We have nothing to write to you about the country but that the farms are all in a very thriving state and produces fine crops. We have sent this few lines to you hoping that that it will not trouble you to much for writing so quick to you. But the country is settling slowly and our children are learning fast, which make us very eager for your assistance, which we hope God's help will be very soon. Our prayers will be for his safe arrival. We have sent you a list of the families that are at present in the settlement so no more present from our humble servants.

	Children
Joseph Gervais X	7
Xavier Laderoute X	1
Etienne Lucier X	6
Pierre Bellique X	3
Charles Rondeau X	3
Charles Plante X	4
Pierre Depot X	1
Andre Picard X	4
Joseph Delard X	5
Louis Forcier X	3
Amable Arquette X	3
Jean-Baptiste Perrault X	2
Joseph Despard X	3
Andre Longtain X	4
Jean-Baptiste Desportes X	8
William Johnson X	2
Charles Chata (Charpentier?) X	
William Mearty X	

ME: LUCIER, Etienne PARISH: Lachine ENTERED SERVICE: ca. 1824 DATES:

›ointments & Service fit Year* Outfit year runs from 1 June to 31 May	Position	Post	District	HBCA Reference
th West Company				
3		Astoria (former Pacific Fur Co.)		F.4/61 fo. 3
3-1814	Hunter	Fort William		F.4/61 fo. 7
ìson's Bay Company				
4-1830	Freeman			B.239/g/4-16, B.223/g/1
0-1831	Trapper		Southern Expedition	B.223/g/2
1-1836	Free Trapper			B.239/g/11-15
6-1843	Willamette Settler			B.239/g/17-22, B.223/g/3-7
3-1844	does not appear			B.239/g/23, B.223/g/8

ation on F.4/61 fo. 7 indicates that North West Co. did not have any agreement "whatever" with Lucier.

cording to the reminiscences of [Donald] Manson's daughter Anna (Mrs. Tremewan)(see Oregon Historical Quarterly, IV, 261-4), her mother was a ghter of Etienne Lucier of French Prairie, Marion County, Oregon. Anna's Brothers were Donald, James, William and Stephen; and her sisters were ›ella and Lizzie."
ken from Hudson's Bay Record Society, Vol. XVIII p. 241.

also H.B.R.S. Vols. IV p. 173, and XXIII

Josiah Markham:

by: Lee Croson Casazza

My third great grandfather, Josiah Markham was born circa 1790 in Bedford County, Virginia, the third son of John Markham and Jenny Eads. His father, John Markham, was a veteran of the Revolutionary War who enlisted in Prince Edward County, Virginia as a noncommissioned officer.

Josiah was one of three brothers who served together during the war of 1812. His two older brothers, James and Nathaniel, were in the same battalion in Fort Norfolk, Virginia. Josiah was discharged on April 9, 1814, having served as a corporal and artillery soldier of Captain William Tibbs' artillery battalion of the Virginia Militia.

The Virginia militia units were called to Norfolk in 1814 after the U.S. frigate Constellation was trying to get to sea after having repairs completed in Baltimore, Maryland. Having arrived in the Hampton Roads area, also known as Tidewater, at the same time as the British blockading fleet of a few thousand men, she was forced to retreat up the river to Norfolk. On June 22, 1813, a British landing crew rowed ashore on the western side of Craney Island. The American artillery on watch with a 15-star and 15-stripe American flag nailed to a pole, saved Norfolk and Portsmouth by firing with deadly accuracy and drove the British back. Unfortunately, the British succeeded in burning the town of Hampton on June 25 and continued their blockade of the Chesapeake Bay. Craney Island was the scene of Virginia's only land battle during the War of 1812. One interesting fact is Craney Island has no cranes. Early settlers on the Elizabeth River mistook the nesting herons for cranes, and the name continues to this day.

The potential danger with the location of the British fleet in the Bay caused most militia to extend their service. Discipline was strictly enforced but garrison duty became increasingly dull. As the end of the second period of enlistment approached, boredom and alcohol began to take its toll.

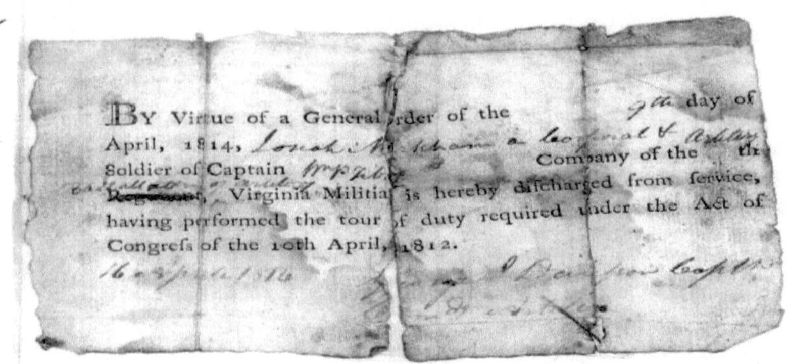

BY Virtue of a General Order of the [illegible] day of April, 1814, [illegible] Company of the [illegible] Soldier of Captain [illegible] Virginia Militia is hereby discharged from service, having performed the tour of duty required under the Act of Congress of the 10th April, 1812.

Between February 27th and March 4th of 1814, there were ten court-martials at Fort Norfolk. Half of those court-martials were the result from "sleeping on post". This was in part because officers did not enforce the requirement for sentinels to stand while on guard. Once tired or bored, it didn't take long for them to nod off. From testimony, it appears that the most convincing evidence was the fact that the reporting officer was able to take the guard's gun without awakening him. When found guilty, soldiers were sentenced to wear a ball and chain for a few hours a day. The rest of the court-martials were a result of "riotous & disorderly conduct". In one instance, Captain Tibbs, an officer of the guard, returned from testifying at a court-martial to find a corporal along with other soldiers and prisoners "very intoxicated and disorderly". The corporal was forced to stand on a narrow block of wood four feet high, on one foot alternately for twenty minutes with his arms extended. After that punishment, he received 20 cobbs on his bare posterior and then put to hard labor with a ball and chain for twenty days and his ration of spirits stopped for the remainder of his service.

Cobbing was a punishment that consisted of striking a prisoner with a flat piece of board with a handle and often perforated with auger holes.

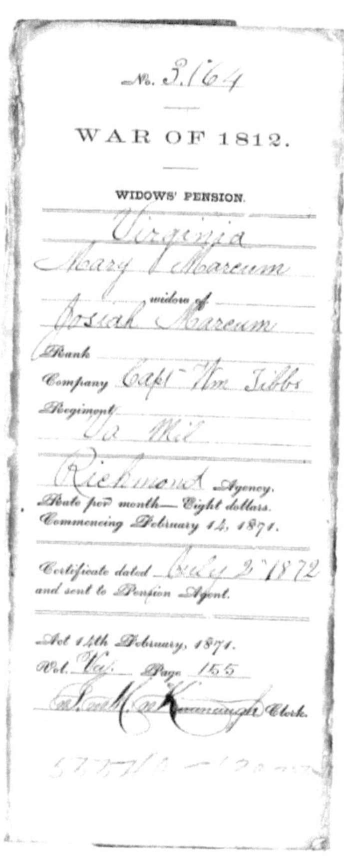

No. 3164

WAR OF 1812.

WIDOWS' PENSION.

Virginia

Mary L Marcum

widow of

Josiah Marcum

Rank

Company Capt Wm Tibbs

Regiment

Va Mil

Richmond Agency.

Rate per month— Eight dollars.

Commencing February 14, 1871.

Certificate dated July 2" 1872

and sent to Pension Agent.

Act 14th February, 1871.

Vol. Va. Page 155

Clerk.

After his discharge, Josiah returned home to Botetourt County, Virginia and married Mary "Polly" Bales, also a child of a Revolutionary Patriot. Around 1820 they migrated to Lee County, Virginia where they raised 12 children. Josiah died on October 7, 1842 at approximately the age of 52. Polly collected his pension commencing February 14, 1874 of $8.00 a month. She died on Mary 15, 1877.

Fortunately, I did not find Josiah Markham or his brothers in the court-martial records. Unfortunately, it would have given me more personal information on my War of 1812 ancestor. I take great pride in knowing that Josiah loved our country and followed in his father's patriotic footsteps.

William Mason:

by: Sandra Warren

1760 – 1830; William Mason fought in the Revolutionary War, enlisting when he was only sixteen as a private in the Army under Col. Hookum, and was later commissioned Major for meritorious service.

During the Indian Wars, in the Ohio Territory, William Mason served under General Josiah Harmar in the fall of 1790. Harmar's army set out to face the Indians to the north but, after a great loss of men, the survivors returned to Fort Washington and the first white settlers continued to live in fear of the victorious Indians. Success did not come until 1795 when the army defeated the Indians and the Treaty of Greenville was signed and settlers began to prepare the land for farming.

Before the declaration of war against England in June, 1812, the people of Southwestern Ohio were frequently alarmed with reports of Indian incursions. The battle of Tippecanoe was fought November 7, 1811. The Indians were defeated but until the commencement of the war with England, the Government was constantly engaged in negotiations with them to prevent more hostilities.

During the year of 1812, many councils were held for the purpose of securing friendly relations with the Indian chiefs; these were not successful. Although their situation was giving rise to feeling of uneasiness for the safety of their homes, the great majority of the people of Warren County, Ohio were in favor of the war with England. On the reception of the news of the formal declaration of war, the people held meetings, passed resolutions of approval, and took steps to respond to the call of the troops.

They received the news that General Hull and his army were prisoners of the enemy and that the British and their Indian allies were marching to meet them. This produced great concern throughout the communities. So strong a feeling of patriotism pervaded the country at that time that it appeared as if every able-bodied man who could possibly raise a horse and a gun was on the move for the frontier. This included William Mason who enlisted for the War of 1812 at the age of 52, a bit older than his fellow recruits.

William Mason served for only a short time and then paid a man named Solsberry to be a substitute for him. Mason outfitted Solsberry for the war and supported the man's wife and four children for the duration.

William Mason was my grandfather, Delmar Michael Crain's great- great grandfather.

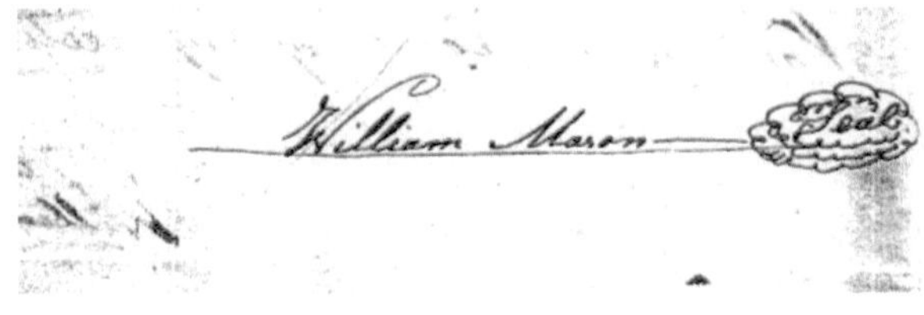

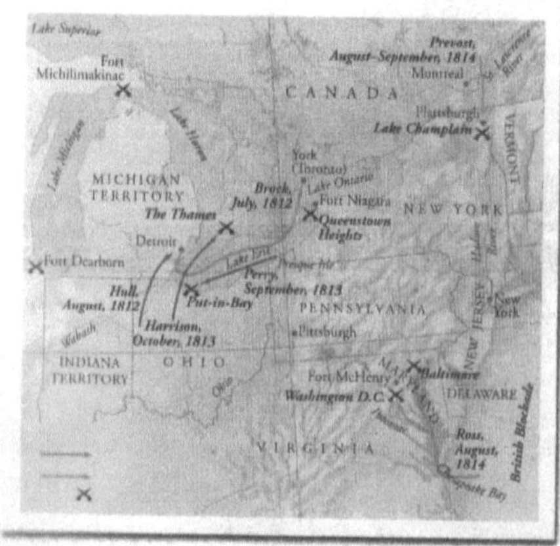

The map shows the many fronts on which the land war of 1812 was fought. While the U. S. Army sought to attack Canada and control the Great Lakes, the British Navy sacked Washington and shot up Fort McHenry in Baltimore, Maryland.

*

NAME Mason, William 315

AGENCY OF PAYMENT Philadelphia Pa

DATE OF ACT 1818

DATE OF PAYMENT 4th ~~2nd~~ qr 1822

DATE OF DEATH

last FINAL PAYMENT VOUCHER RECEIVED FROM THE GENERAL ACCOUNTING OFFICE

GENERAL SERVICES ADMINISTRATION GSA DC 70-7038 GSA FORM DEC 68 7016

Taken from ***The History of Warren County, Ohio***, W.H. Beers & Co, reprinted 1971.

DEERFIELD TOWNSHIP. 993

of Major William Mason. After the celebration of this event he located on land adjoining the village of Mason. He has been successful during life, and his farm of 440 acres attests the fact. He has been no political aspirant, caring nothing for the bauble of office, and with the exception of one year he served as Justice of the Peace, has held no other office. He has been a member of the Mason Horse Rangers for thirty years. Major William Mason and wife, Sarah Murphy, were parents of Mrs. Wikoff; he was born in Pennsylvania, and afterwards removed to Palmyra, Tenn., from whence he came to Ohio, about 1798, and first settled on the Little Miami river, near Madisonville, Ohio. Here he lost his first wife Mary McClellan, and soon after came to this township, in which he bought 36 acres, the present site of Mason. By his first wife he had two children, viz.—Maria and Samuel. By the second four children, viz.: Cynthia, Sarah, William and Elizabeth. At the age of sixteen he entered in the war of the Revolution, and served under Col. Hookum; for meritorious service was commissioned Major. He also enlisted in 1812, but only served a short time. He was much noted for his liberality, and at his death willed to the village of Mason 40 acres of land.

JOHN C. WODREY, farmer; P. O. Foster's Crossing. The gentleman whose name we present at the head of this sketch, is one of the prominent and

Taken from ***Around Mason, Ohio***, Rose Marie Springman 1982

1812

Deerfield Township was fully represented in the War of 1812. Twenty-six men's names were recorded as having been involved in the battles to the north and northeast of their homes to route out the British. They were Joseph Coddington and his two sons, Samuel and Freeman, Mason, Philip and James Seward, Brazilla Clark, Richard Cox, James Johnson, John Parkhill, John Lowe, John Patton, William Mason, James Striker, Robert Doan, Patrick Shaw, Jedediah Tingle, David and Fred Briney, George and John Cline, Caliph Leonard, Dick Compton, Byron Williams, Sam Harris and Nicholas Rynearson. Many of these were older married men and perhaps some served their term as did William Mason, who, at age 52 himself, paid a man named Solsberry to be a substitute for him. Mason outfitted Solsberry for the war and supported the man's wife and four children for the duration.

In February James Leonard and Jane Biggs were married and so were Absolom Fox and Jane McFarland.

John and Catherine Kitchel Leonard came to the area from New Jersey. He was 31 and she 24. Both had relatives who had already settled in Warren County. Some of their grandchildren continued the westward move, one taking an active part in the Gold Rush in California in the early 1850s and another settling in South Dakota.

Map of Mason, Ohio which was named after William Mason after his death.

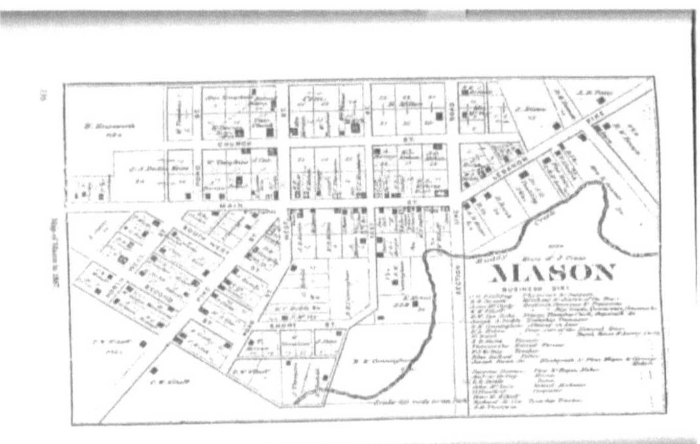

In the year 2015, Mason, Ohio will celebrate their bicentennial. At that time, there will be a plaque showing the descendants of William Mason presented to the city.

Maj William Mason

Memorial

Learn about sponsoring this memorial...

Birth: 1760
Death: 1830

Major in the Revolutionary War.
Served also against the Miami Indians and in the War of 1812.
Founder of Palmyra, Ohio,
later, in his honor, named Mason.

On June 1, 1803, Revolutionary War veteran William Mason paid $1,700 at auction to purchase 640 acres of land in what is now downtown Mason. In 1815, he platted 16 lots on this land and named the village "Palmyra." In 1832, 2 years after the death of William Mason and according to his will, over 40 more lots were platted on the north, south, and west of Palmira. When the plat was officially recorded, the name of the village was listed as "Palmyra."

In 1835, a petition was sent to the federal post office to correct the name of the town. It had been listed as Kirkwood, possibly an error because the postmaster at the time was William Kirkwood. When village officials were informed that there was another Palmyra in Ohio, the name was officially changed to "Mason." Mason remained a small farming community for another 125 years. In 1970, a year before the town was incorporated to become a city, there were fewer than 5,700 residents. Today, the City of Mason covers over 11,200 acres and is home to nearly 25,000 people and approximately 500 businesses.

Taken from William Mason's niece's journal, as printed in book ***Around Mason, Ohio,*** by Rose Marie Springman, 1982.

1830

At some point during the past years William Mason had moved from his farm to a house south of his town. The house was on Road Street and faced east toward the Muddy Creek. A well from which the water supply was bought up by means of a well sweep was in the yard. In February William Mason died in that well. His granddaughter, Flora Tetrick, was to write in her journal: "Grandfather was drawing water and fell in the well head foremost, struck his head and drowned. Ma had his hat for years, a silk plush colonial style, and the cut in the hat was about four or five inches. He drowned in February." It is said that his mother died the same year at age 90. His young wife had only a few more years to live.

William Mason's will formally gave to his two older children the 100 acre plots he had assigned them two years before. The next item stated: "I give, will and bequeath unto my wife Sally Mason, to my eldest daughter Maria, wife of Lucas D. Leonard, to my son Samuel Mason and to my two younger daughters Cynthia and Sally the whole of the amount of income arising from the sale of lots in the town of Palmyra and also the amount of the sale of lots laid off and sold by my Executors in addition to the number of lots already laid off which I will and direct to be laid to the amount of forty acres to be laid out in such place and in such form as may best suit the prospects of the town, which sums to be divided equally among them, share and share alike."

Mason's wife was further provided for, beyond the widow's one third of the estate according to law, by an item that stated: "I bequeath unto my wife Sally Mason one bay horse (called Rock) and the three milch cows and eight sheep, also the household furniture and kitchen furniture together with the beds and bedding, also twelve hogs, six for killing this fall and six for

stock suitable to be kept over winter. I give and bequeath unto my son Samuel Mason the remainder of the hogs requiring of him to fat the hogs already bequeathed to my wife and to feed in a proper manner such of hers as may be intended to be kept over winter." Possibly Samuel lived on the original family farm and could carry out the last request. However cows, horses, sheep and swine on town lots were the rule at the time rather than the exception and Sally's livestock might have stayed right with her.

The Warren County commissioners exacted a tax of five mills on each dollar of income of each physician in the area. It was estimated that the average doctor had an income of $500 per year at the time. The only doctor listed in 1830 for Deerfield Township was John DeHart.

The newly elected township trustees were James McCowen, John Bigam and James Baxter.

Deborah Monfort, age 19, and Reuben Hoff, age 27, married and settled down to farming. Both had been born in New Jersey and brought by their families at a very early age to Deerfield Township. She was the daughter of Elbert and Nancy Monfort and he the son of John and Ruth Fields Hoff. Deborah was to have ten children and live to the age of 78. Reuben survived her by almost two years and died at the age of 88.

Walter Middleton:

by: Lee Croson Casazza

My third great grandfather, Walter Middleton, Jr. was born about 1795 in Chadwell Station, Lee County, Virginia. He was the son of Walter Middleton, Sr. and Mary Chadwell. According to tradition, "shortly after a buffalo hunt, Walter Sr. died of a heart attack". His will was proved 14 Jul 1795.

Walter never knew his father as he died a few months before his birth. Walter left Lee Co., Virginia as a young man looking for adventure and moved to the part of Knox County, Kentucky which later became Harlan County. Walter married Sarah Turner in Harlan Co., Kentucky. Sarah was the daughter of William Turner and Susannah Bailey. Both of their fathers were Patriots of the Revolutionary War. Walter and Sarah settled, raising their family near Cloverfork in Harlan County. Walter and Sarah had five sons, three of them served their country in the Confederate Army during the Civil War for southern independence. Walter and Sarah had one son-in-law who fought for the south and one son-in-law who fought for the North. Walter died in 1863 at the age of 68 in Harlan County; Sarah died around 1870. One of their sons, James T. Middleton, was killed at the end of the Civil War by a band of men who captured and tortured him. They dismantled his body and stuffed it in a hollow log. He was not found for several years. Luckily his son, Walter Middleton III, was born and married Susan Pope, my great grandparents.

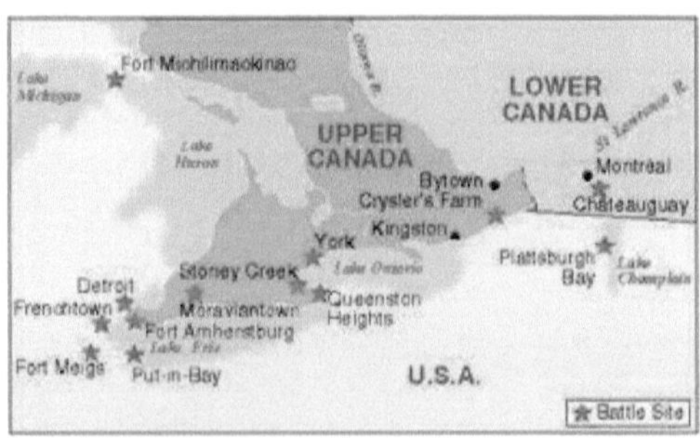

Walter Middleton, Jr. fought in the War of 1812. He was an officer under the command of General William Henry Harrison, who later became our ninth President and fought in the Battle of Thames on October 5, 1813.

This is when Tecumseh, the famous Shawnee Indian Chief, was killed. Story has it that Walter often bragged about firing the shot that killed the famous chief. William H. Harrison led an American force of about 3,000 against a British army of approximately 400 regulars commanded by Gen. Henry A. Procter, reinforced by 1,000 Naive Americans under Chief Tecumseh. After the British were driven from Detroit, Harrison followed their retreating army into Ontario and up the Thames River until General Procter was forced to give battle. A cavalry charge broke the British ranks, and the Native Americans offered the only real resistance. Tecumseh was slain in battle, thus, completely destroying the native confederacy he had raised against the United States and U.S. control in the Northwest was restored.

When Tecumseh was slain, Indians came at night and took his body away. For many years his body had no final resting place. His bones had been moved several times and someone always knew where they were. Finally, in 1931, a resolution had been passed that the bones that had been preserved on Walpole Island were the actual bones of Tecumseh. Money was raised and the bones of the famous old leader were buried and a simple monument was erected over his grave. Today the grave overlooks the St. Clair River near Detroit, Michigan.

If Tecumseh's idea of organizing the various Indian tribes to resist white settlement had succeeded, it would have seriously changed the course of American history. His political skills and charismatic leadership made him a revered figure.

Countless tributes to Tecumseh have appeared over the past two centuries, including the naming of towns and US Navy ships for him. During the American Civil War, William Tecumseh Sherman was a Union general and was given his middle name in honor of Tecumseh because his father respected the Shawnee chief.

One quirk of history became known as "Tecumseh's curse." William Henry Harrison, whose life intertwined with Tecumseh, was elected president in 1840, caught a cold while delivering the longest inauguration address in history, and died a month later.

Thomas Edmund Pearsall:

by: Kimberly Anne Cambern

Thomas Edmund Pearsall was born on July 29, 1778 in Hempstead, Long Island, New York; only three years before the British murdered his father and grandfather.

The parents of Thomas, Edmund Pearsall and Elizabeth Pope, were from long-time families of Long Island and Martha's Vineyard. Elizabeth's husband Edmund Pearsall and father John Pope both served during the Revolutionary War, where they were captured by the British and sent to the infamous prison ship Jersey.

The HMS Jersey was the most notorious of all the prison ships, its inhuman conditions and extremely high death rate, earned it the nickname of "HMS Hell". An American prisoner on the Jersey, Christopher Vail, wrote:

> "When a man died he was carried up on the forecastle and laid there until the next morning at 8 o'clock when they were all lowered down the ship sides by a rope round them in the same manner as tho' they were beasts. There was 8 died of a day while I was there. They were carried on shore in heaps and hove out the boat on the wharf, then taken across a hand barrow, carried to the edge of the bank, where a hole was dug 1 or 2 feet deep and all hove in together."

Robert Sheffield, a prisoner on another ship, also writes:

> "The heat was so intense that (the hot sun shining all day on deck) they were all naked, which also served the well to get rid of vermin, but the sick were eaten up alive. Their sickly countenances, and ghastly looks were truly horrible; some swearing and blaspheming; others crying, praying, and wringing their hands; and stalking about like ghosts; others delirious, raving and storming,--all panting for breath; some dead, and corrupting. The air was so foul that at times a lamp could not be kept burning, by reason of which the bodies were not missed until they had been dead ten days."

In 1781, to save their family members, both the Pearsalls and Popes, raised the funds to ransom their loved ones from the Jersey. The sum of the ransom is unknown, but it was believed to have been substantial. Once the money was paid, they were both released, but unknown to the families, the British had poisoned both men before they let them go. Therefore, Elizabeth Pope Pearsall was left without her husband and father, and three-year-old Thomas, along with his three siblings, were left fatherless.

By 1784, Thomas' mother Elizabeth had married one of her cousins, Joseph Tobey, by 1795, they had moved to Smyrna, Chenango Co., N. Y., where they were among the earliest settlers. Joseph came to Smyrna first in 1795 with Joseph Porter (Elizabeth's older sister's husband) but did not bring his family until the next year. In March, Joseph brought Elizabeth and the six children, two of theirs and four from her marriage to Edmund. They made the journey with a yoke of oxen and two cows, which were hitched, miss-matched, to a sled that held the household goods and the children. It is said that when they arrived at Pleasant Brook it was swollen and full of running ice from the spring floods making the passage dangerous, forcing them to cross on wet logs with their belongings strapped to their backs.

Elizabeth sat upon one of those logs, wondering about her fate; she had left a comfortable home and family for the wilderness of "Indians and wild beasts". Nevertheless, they were here for better or for worse!

When the War of 1812 started, Thomas Edmund Pearsall was one of the first to enlist. He left his wife, Philothe Warren Pearsall, his four children, Mary Ann, Simon, Darius Warren, Emma Elvira and his home in Cooperstown to fight the British; he never came back. Elizabeth Pope Pearsall Tobey had now lost a father, a husband and a son to the British.

Zalmond Randall:

By: Caron Anderson, Randi Anderson Brown and Roger Scott Anderson

Zalmon(d) Randall (born 26 April 1798 in Otsego, NY, died 13 March 1854 in Monmouth, Indiana) was a Fife Major in the 13th New York Infantry Regiment, Roll Box 171, Roll Exct 602 during the War of 1812. Zalmond was the son of Joshua Randall (1758-1828), Fife Colonel in the American Revolution and is part of the William Randall (1609-1693) of Scituate Family Tree.

The 13th Regiment of NY Infantry was formed July 16, 1798 during the first post war expansion of the US Army (following the American Revolution). The 13th Regiment was then mustered out on January 11, 1800.

During the War of 1812, the 13th Regiment of NY Infantry was consolidated with the 5th Infantry and took part in a series of long engagements. Most of these battles took place in the Niagara frontier in Upstate New York. The unit is most noted for the Battle of Plattsburgh.

Following the war, Zalmond moved west with his parents and siblings, eventually settling in Michigan with his own family.
In the book, Randall and Allied Families, it is noted that Zalmond's brother Alvan (Alvin), living in Franklin County, Ohio, "furnished lighting to neighbors to celebrate Jackson's Victory at New Orleans".

Captain Seth Ranney:

by: Robin Savage

The Ranney family joined the long history and procession of settlers coming to what is now Oneida County, coming from Connecticut in 1785 or 1786, and located in the shadow of Fort Stanwix. They were all related to each other by blood, or connected by marriage. Their names were as follows: Willett Ranney, Sr., with a family of eleven children, all grown to maturity, and most if not all married; Seth Ranney, one of the sons, with wife and children, located northeast of the present Rome Court House on or near the site of the late residence of G. N. Bissell. Willett Ranney, Jr., another son, and his family; also Nathaniel Gilbert and David I. Andrus, both of whom had married in the Ranney family, and had been in the War of the Revolution.[i] Many of the Ranney named served in the Revolution from Massachusetts and Connecticut, and the name is an eminent one among families of New England.

The years 1812, 1813 and 1814 covered the War of 1812. They were busy and important ones for the Mohawk Valley which was again the great warpath of the nation, as it had been during all of America's wars, from the outbreak of King William's War in 1689 to 1814, a period of 125 years. Although our school histories give much attention to the capture of Washington and the battle of New Orleans, the main fighting of the War of 1812 was done on the Niagara, St. Lawrence and Lake Champlain frontiers. As in our Colonial Wars and the Revolution, the Mohawk-St. Lawrence-Champlain triangle became the defensive military key position of the United States. Troops for the New York frontiers were constantly passing over the Mohawk turnpikes while military supplies and ordnance went westward over the river. The Scotia campground was used by American troops during the War of 1812, just as it had been previously during the Revolution and the Colonial Wars. The Mohawk Valley militia, in large numbers, was actively engaged in this war generally on the Niagara and St. Lawrence frontiers.[ii]

Willett Ranney, Sr. was born 28 March 1731 in Upper House, Middletown, CT and died 1818 at Smithville, Jefferson Co. NY. He was a patriot (see Fonda List for his extensive service) and DAR proven patriot.

Seth Ranney, son of Willett Ranney and Mary Butler was born 21 Jan 1761 at Upper Houses and died 21 July 1839 and is buried in Ogdensburg Cemetery, St. Lawrence Co., NY. He married Eleanor Matthews, who died 12 March 1813 at 50 years. In June of 1790, Willett Ranney, Jr. leased 100 acres from then Governor Clinton in Wright's Settlement next to the 100-acre settlement of his brother, Seth. Seth Ranney erected the first 2-story framehouse in Rome. In 1792, it was used as a tavern by John Barnard, and in 1793 the first store was opened in it. In this year, he was one of the 15 charter members of a Masonic Lodge organized and located in the township of Paris - the first lodge in Central New York.[iii] The first town meeting was held in April of 1793 at his house (Town Meeting Minutes), in the house "lately occupied by Seth Ranney." Brother James Ranney was present at that same meeting. Known as Capt. Seth Ranney, having served in the War of 1812, he resided in Canada for a few years and then returned to Ogdensburg, NY. In 1801, both Ranneys moved on to Saratoga, NY. He had a farm on the St. Lawrence River and also kept a hotel.

Among the early settlers in Rome, NY, previous to 1800, were John Barnard, George Huntington, Joshua Hathaway, Dr. Stephen White, Henry Huntington, Rozel Fellows, Matthew Brown, Bill Smith, Seth Ranney, Matthew Brown, Jr., David Brown, Ebenezer, Daniel W. and Thomas Wright, Thomas Selden, Solomon and John Williams, Peter Colt, William Coibraith, Abijah and Clark Putnam, Caleb Reynolds, Rufus Eaton, Thomas Gilbert, Moses Fish, Stephen Lampman, Jeremiah Steves, Annin Wiggins and John Niles.[iv]

Children of Seth Ranney and Eleanor Matthews:

i. George Ranney born 1780 was married three times and died 27 May 1860
ii. Lois Ranney who married Sylvester Gilbert of Ogdensburg
iii. Betsy Ranney who married James Chambers and moved to North Carolina
iv. Belinda Ranney who was born 6 Dec. 1791 and married Henry Lum
v. Clarissa Ranney who married 1) David Lum and 2) Josiah Perry

At the close of the French War, there were in the valley army fortifications at Fort Stanwix (now Rome, erected 1758). Fort Stanwix, or Schuyler, of the Revolution was an American Army stronghold built on the original earthwork constructed on the present site of Rome by General John Stanwix in 1758. In 1776, Col. Dayton evidently did little but make this post tenable for a comparatively small garrison. Most of the real strengthening of the fort was done under Col. Willett's direction in 1777 upon the approach of St. Leger's army.

The original Fort Stanwix, as repaired by Col. Dayton, is described as follows:

> Fort Stanwix cost 60,000 pounds and was originally constructed on the most approved scientific principles of engineering, "having four bastions surrounded by a broad ditch, eighteen feet deep with a covert way and glaces. In the center of the ditch was a row of perpendicular pickets and a horizontal row from the ramparts. Col. Bradstreet and a detachment of his American militiamen assisted in building this famous post upon their return from the capture of Fort Frontenac (Kingston) in Canada in 1758.

Fort Herkimer, Fort Dayton and Fort Stanwix figure prominently in the invasion of St. Leger's army, the siege of Fort Stanwix and the battle of Oriskany (Aug. 6, 1777). Fort Stanwix was abandoned in 1781, after being severely damaged by fire.[v]

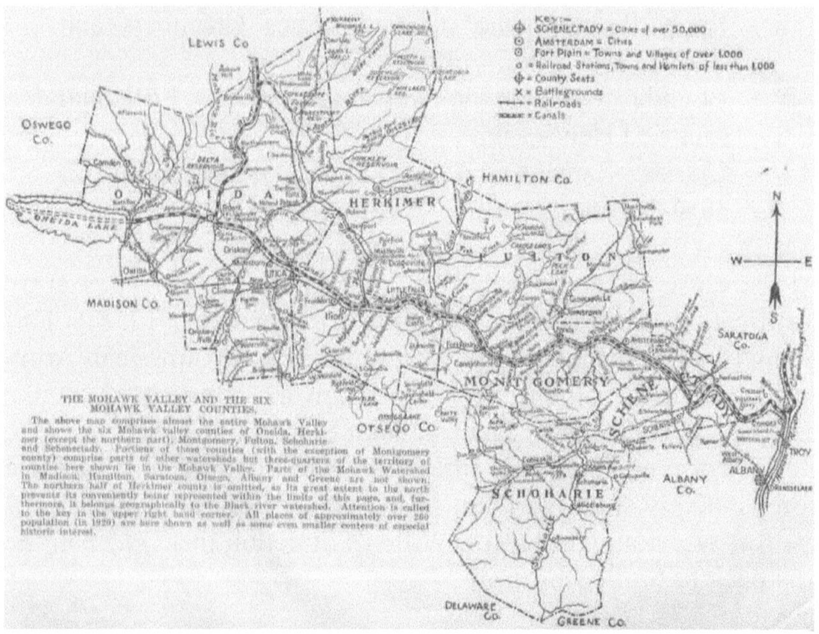

The above map comprises almost the entire Mohawk Valley and shows the six Mohawk Valley counties of Oneida, Herkimer (except the northern part), Montgomery, Fulton, Schoharie and Schenectady. Portions of these counties (with the exception of Montgomery county) comprise parts of other watersheds but three-quarters of the territory of counties here shown lie in the Mohawk Valley. Parts of the Mohawk Watershed in Madison, Hamilton, Saratoga, Otsego, Albany and Greene are not shown. The northern half of Herkimer county is omitted, as its great extent to the north prevents its conveniently being represented within the limits of this page, and, furthermore, it belongs geographically to the Black river watershed. Attention is called to the key in the upper right hand corner. All places of approximately over 200 population (in 1920) are here shown as well as some even smaller centers of especial historic interest.

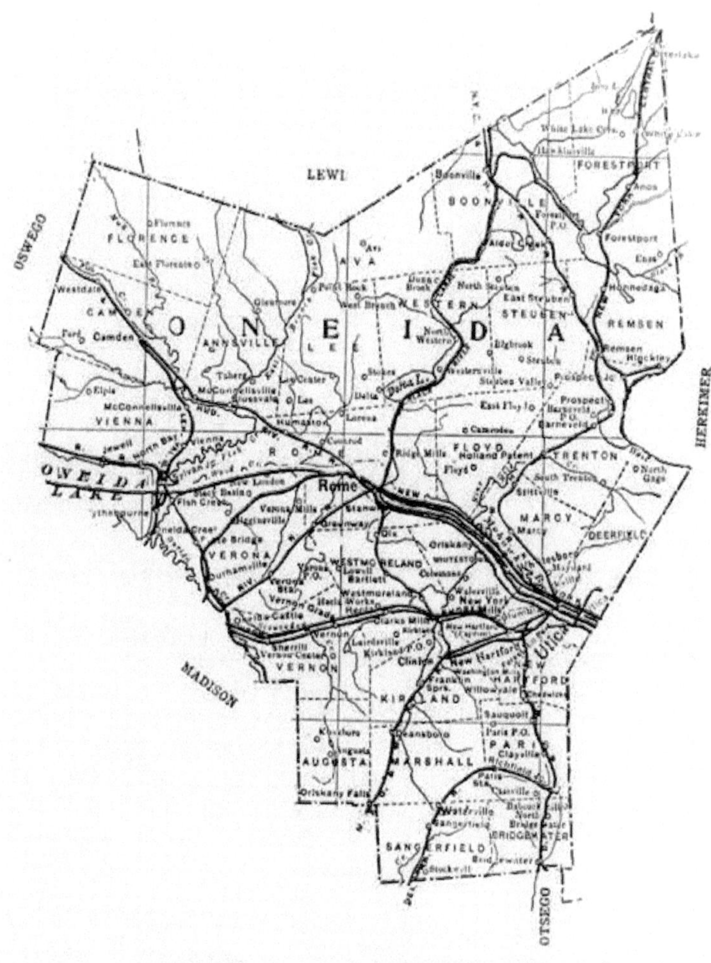

Map of Oneida County, showing Townships. From the *Agricultural Manual of New York State*.

Painting: Farm Slopes of the Mohawk Valley. Painted by Edward Gay, published by courtesy of Bartlett Arkell.

This beautiful landscape represents the Mohawk Valley Hills near Canajoharie at harvest time. In the distance are the river and flats at Sprakers with the Noses looming over them. The picture was painted in 1877 by Edward Gay, a distinguished American landscape artist.

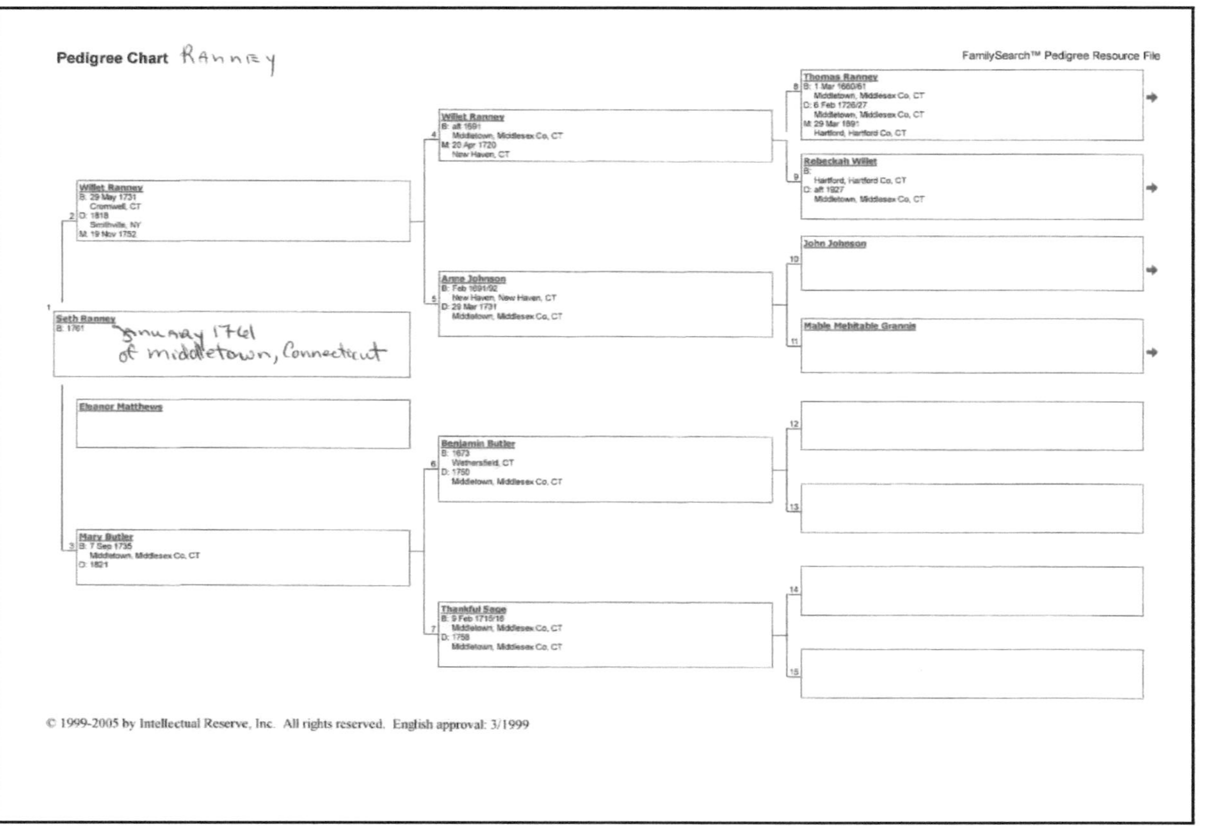
Pedigree Chart Ranney
FamilySearch™ Pedigree Resource File
1 Seth Ranney
B: 1761
January 1761
of Middletown, Connecticut
2 Willet Ranney
B: 29 May 1731
Cromwell, CT
D: 1818
Smithville, NY
M: 19 Nov 1752
Eleanor Matthews
3 Mary Butler
B: 7 Sep 1735
Middletown, Middlesex Co, CT
D: 1821
4 Willet Ranney
B: aft 1691
Middletown, Middlesex Co, CT
M: 20 Apr 1720
New Haven, CT
5 Anne Johnson
B: Feb 1691/92
New Haven, New Haven, CT
D: 29 Mar 1731
Middletown, Middlesex Co, CT
6 Benjamin Butler
B: 1673
Wethersfield, CT
D: 1750
Middletown, Middlesex Co, CT
7 Thankful Sage
B: 9 Feb 1715/16
Middletown, Middlesex Co, CT
D: 1758
Middletown, Middlesex Co, CT
8 Thomas Ranney
B: 1 Mar 1660/61
Middletown, Middlesex Co, CT
D: 6 Feb 1726/27
Middletown, Middlesex Co, CT
M: 29 Mar 1691
Hartford, Hartford Co, CT
9 Rebeckah Willet
B:
Hartford, Hartford Co, CT
D: aft 1927
Middletown, Middlesex Co, CT
10 John Johnson
11 Mable Mehitable Grannis
12
13
14
15
© 1999-2005 by Intellectual Reserve, Inc. All rights reserved. English approval: 3/1999

DECLARATION OF SURVIVING SOLDIER FOR PENSION.

ACT OF FEBRUARY 14, 1871.

State of Ohio
Geauga County. } ss:

On this 18th day of April, A. D. one thousand eight hundred and seventy One, personally appeared before me (1) Judge of Probate Court of the said County, a court of record within and for the County and State aforesaid (2) Josiah Bail, aged 82 years, a resident of Chardon, County of Geauga, and State of Ohio, who, being duly sworn according to law, declares that he is not married; (3) *that his wife's name was* Amna Edmunds *to whom he was married at* Litchfield Conn N.Y. *on the* 16 *day of* October 1816; that he served the full period of sixty days in the (4) Military service of the United States in the war of 1812; that he is the identical Josiah Bail who (5) Enlisted in Captain Ranneys Company, Fourth Regiment Conn Inf, Brigade, Division, at Litchfield in the State of Conn on the 4th day of August 1808, and was honorably discharged at Burlington Vt on the 4th day of August, 1813, that (6) That he enlisted for the period of five years and served under Captain Ranney until he was promoted & then Captain Bunny commanded said Company.

That under act of Sept 28 1850 he applied for & received 160 acres of Bounty Land said Warrant was No 4320

that he at no time, during the late rebellion against the authority of the United States, adhered to the cause of the enemies of the Government, giving them aid and comfort, or exercised the functions of any office whatever under any authority or pretended authority in hostility to the United States; and that he will support the Constitution of the United States; *that he is not in receipt of a pension under any previous act*; (7)

that he makes this declaration for the purpose of being placed on the pension-roll of the United States under the provisions of the Act of February 14, 1871; and he hereby constitutes and appoints, with full power of substitution and revocation, **CHARLES C. TUCKER, of Washington, D. C.**, his true and lawful Attorney, to prosecute his claim and obtain the pension certificate that may be issued; that his post office is at Chardon, County of Geauga, State of Ohio, and that his domicil or place of abode is Chardon O.

(8) Josiah Bail

ATTEST:
J. Hathaway
Tilden W Porter

[i]This information is from Vol. II, pp. 1175-1183 of *History of the Mohawk Valley: Gateway to the West 1614-1925*, edited by Nelson Greene (Chicago: The S. J. Clarke Publishing Company, 1925). It is in the Reference collection of the Schenectady County Public Library at R 974.7 G81h.

ii Ibid.

[iii] Source: Middletown CT Upper Houses, History of the North Society of Middletown, CT. from 1650-1800 with genealogical and biographical chapters on early families, Charles Collard Adams, New York: Grafton Press 1908, (transcribed by Liz Mathews); source provided by Marilyn Sapienza, msapienza@cox.net , contributor to Jefferson County Genweb Page.

[iv] Source: History of Rome NY

[v] This information is from Vol. II, pp. 1184-1196 of *History of the Mohawk Valley: Gateway to the West 1614-1925*, edited by Nelson Greene (Chicago: The S. J. Clarke Publishing, Company 1925).

Asahel Roundy:

by: Phyllis Toomey

July 29, 1784 – October 22, 1855; It was a cold October blustery day but not as bitter as upper New York would become later this fall of 1814. Captain Asahel Roundy was leading the Sixth Militia of New York 95 miles north to Sackets Harbor, New York on Lake Ontario. Lake Ontario was the boundary between British-loyal Canada and the newly formed United States. He was proud to serve his new state. He had moved to Spafford, New York in 1807 when he was 22 years of age with New York becoming his new home. His mother, brothers and sisters had followed him to Spafford.

As he rode, he thought about the family he had left behind in Spafford. He was only thirty years old, being born July 29, 1784. He was born in Vermont to Uriah Roundy and Lucretia Needham. He had named his first child, a daughter, Lucretia after his mother. His daughter was only 4 years old, with three younger siblings: Gordon who would soon be three, Mary Ann who was almost two years old, and little Lizana who was just nine months. His wife, Hannah Weston, whom he married in 1809, originally came from New Hampshire. She, too, had moved to Spafford in her youth. She had been a teacher at the local Spafford school; she was a great wife and mother. It was hard to say good bye but he knew he must.

The United States had established its independence 36 years before in 1776 but England continued to do battle, trying to assert its dominance over the continent. In 1812 war broke out again with a vengeance with James Madison declaring war in June of 1812. It was the first time that war was actually declared by the new country, in spite of all the previous battles. The British army joined with the Canadian troops. Adding to its forces were the native Indians who had been promised their own nation if this triad power could defeat the upstart Americans.

For Captain Roundy, the decision to join the militia was one of duty. His father, grandfather and three uncles had fought for independence in the Revolutionary War. He could not, he would not allow their sacrifices to go unmet by his generation. The existence of this new country was constantly being threatened. But, in 1812, the northern boundary states did consider Canada a major threat. The British were distracted by a war with France and it was assumed that there was little energy or commitment to do battle along the Great Lakes borders. But this assumption turned out to be falsely optimistic. On December 30, 1813, the British/Canadian armies attacked and burned Buffalo to the ground. Buffalo was only 140 miles away from Spafford as the crow flies. The threat was real.

He was also concerned about his livelihood and his continuing ability to provide for his quickly growing family. He had purchased considerable real estate in the eastern part of Spafford and would sell parcels of land to new settlers. In fact, he had laid out many of the roads in that area. It was important that stability return to New York so that immigrants and those living on the eastern coast continue to move west. Asahel had become a prominent member of the Spafford community. When he was notified that he would need to take command and march to Sackets Harbor, he was attending the Board of Supervisors meeting for Onondaga County. He was a tall man, six foot tall, well proportioned, athletic and well spoken, a natural leader. So, based on his strong patriotic heritage and his own commitment to his community, Asahel was dedicated to his country's and town's survival.

Sackets Harbor, New York was a major shipbuilding location for the American navy. It was a strategic location, being at the eastern end of Lake Ontario. In an attempt to destroy the American shipyard, a British-Canadian force launched an attack on Sackets Harbor on May 29, 1813. At that time, the majority of the American forces were across Lake Ontario attacking Fort

George. The primary role of the 6th Militia was to provide a strong defense and to assist with the staging of supplies and armaments.

Fortunately, the service of the Captain Roundy and his men was short-lived. His company was discharged back home on November 22, 1814. In Ghent, Belgium a treaty was reached in December 1814. However, news of the treaty did not reach parts of the United States until much later. In fact, Andrew Jackson won the Battle of New Orleans in January 1815 after peace had been officially reached. And in late 1814 in Sackets Harbor, ironically, the shipyard was building a state of the art new ship that was named The New Orleans. It was not finished until after the war was over and served for many decades.

Captain Roundy returned to Spafford. His family and his reputation continued to grow throughout his life. His fourth daughter, Nancy was born in 1816. She was followed by four brothers: Asahel Madison in 1818, Uriah in 1819, Franklin 1822 and Charles in 1923. Asahel's prominence in Spafford expanded as well. He held many public offices including commissioner of the poor, assessor, pathmaster and supervisor. He was a Justice of the Peace for over 25 years. Because of his knowledge of the law, fairness and ability to persuade he was frequently asked to represent parties in a legal dispute, both sides: defense and offense. His schooling had been acquired only in common schools but his retentive memory and the command of the language garnered him the reputation of a great speaker.

Captain Roundy was a soldier, politician and a father. But the stories that were documented were ones that spoke of his compassion and fairness and respect for all men. When Asahel first moved to the wilderness of Spafford, a neighbor was building a log home when a misplaced log rolled on the man and broke his leg. Asahel carried him on his back for a mile and a half up a very steep grade to his own house where the man was cared for until he recovered.

At another time, early in Spafford's history, burials took place in open pasture land on the east side of town. The owner of the property refused one family the right to bury on that land. An appeal for assistance was made to Asahel. He bought an acre of the land and allowed the family to bury their family member. That cemetery exists until this day. Captain Asahel Roundy was also a kind and fair man. Asahel's children moved across the expanding country. His son, Gordon, relocated to Illinois and married Maria Kimball in Naperville. It was one of the very first weddings in that territory. Gordon's great great grandchild is Phyllis Hadley Toomey and his great great great grandchild is Mary Jo Toomey Callahan.

Captain Allen Scroggs:

by: Lisa Fowler

1773-1839; Allen Scroggs was born in 1773 in Big Spring Cumberland County, Pennsylvania, the son of Alexander and Rachel Scroggs. Alexander, Allen, and another brother came over to the United States from Scotland settling in Cumberland Co. about 1740. Not that much is known about the family occupation but it seems that they were farmers owning land in Cumberland Co.

Captain Allen Scroggs married Margaret Craig in the Big Springs Presbyterian Church on September 22, 1795 in Newville, Cumberland Co, PA. I don't have a date for the death of Margaret Craig, but Captain Allen married again, this time to Miriam Porter. She and Allen had the following children: Alexander, Rebecca, Miriam, Allen, Joseph and John. Miriam died around 1816. It is not known why the family emigrated to Ohio but son Allen was born in Steubenville, OH in 1803.

Ohio's Roster of the War of 1812 consisted of a total of 26,280 men who enlisted from Ohio to assist the nation in this war. They comprised 3 regiments, 464 companies, 13 cavalry troops and 1 artillery battery. Captain John Scroggs is shown in the Roster of Ohio Soldier in the War of 1812 as having his own company, serving under Lt. Colonel John Andrew's Ohio Regiment, the date of service being from September 21 until November 30, 1812. These men were probably from Jefferson County.

I was not able to discern exactly where this regiment served but from the following information taken from the 1812 Genealogy forum I have found some history. The defense of northeastern Ohio was organized with one militia brigade under the command of Brigadier General Simon Perkins and another militia brigade under the Command of Brigadier. General Beall.

General Beall's force was made up of one regiment from the first brigade headquartered in Jefferson County, and the other regiment from his own second brigade from Columbiana County. The two regiments met in Canton, moved on to Wooster in Wayne County where the brigade erected a blockhouse and established a camp called Camp Christmas. From Wooster, the militia companies were sent to the various settlements within the county where they built additional blockhouses for the protection of the settlers. Along the way, the companies either built new roads or improved existing roads so that the wagons could pass. The enlistment periods were for very short periods and Captain Allen's company only served 3 months at a time according to enlistment records.

Captain Allen Scroggs is buried in Woodland Cemetery, in Zenia, Greene Co., OH. Some of this information is from a letter his granddaughter Lena wrote at the age of 88 in the year 1932. Her father could remember Captain. Allen, going to and then coming home from the war.

And...There Were Those Who Did Not Serve:

by: Margaret Ernest

When I first started looking at the possibility of some of my ancestors serving our country during The War of 1812, I was rather confident that I would find at least one or two who might qualify. As I got into the research, I was frustrated by the fact that I found no one who qualified. Finally, I looked at that war in a little more detail and found that there were many reasons why "my" men did not serve.

First of all, this war was quite region specific. The major conflicts took place in discrete places, usually centered around waterways. In the northern United States, where most of my ancestors lived, the conflicts were centered around the connecting waterways of the Great Lakes westward from the St. Lawrence River. A rather small area of Lake Champlain was also involved.

Other conflicts occurred up and down the Atlantic Coast and, of course, in New Orleans. However, some of my ancestors lived great distances away from these areas and were only peripherally involved in this conflict. This was the case with my paternal grandmother's family in northern Vermont. The distance may only have been a few miles but we need to keep in mind that our country was young and our roads were only poorly developed at best. Railroads were a distant dream and the Erie Canal was not to be even in the planning for another decade. Travel was a challenge in the best of times along rough and uncertain roads and paths, on foot, on horseback and by wagon.

Added to these complexities was the environment of an agrarian society conducted in harsh and demanding circumstances. Every instant of the day demanded intense involvement with the crops and animals: sowing, weeding, harvesting, storing. Weather extremes and crop failure were familiar fears.

There was no easily available idle time to be involved with a far-away, hard to get to conflict that did not seem too relevant to everyday life. And there were some very real human factors involved.
The Revolution itself had involved many disparate points of view, and there had been many who had not really wanted independence at the outset. After the battles were fought and won, life had settled into the normal fabric of the time. Farming was the main occupation accompanied by the associated efforts of supporting society's needs. Although not a major part of society, commerce played a major role in the trading, buying and selling of farm products and every day survival.

In northern Vermont, where my great-grandfather's extended family lived for over one hundred years, the animosities of the Revolution had been soon forgotten. Indeed, the physical border between Vermont and lower Quebec was not finally legally settled until 1845. Up until then, the border had varied locations over four or five decades depending on the current attitudes and discussions. It was entirely possible for some to have lived in both Canada and Vermont over that period of time without having physically moved at all. Added to this confusion was the fact that many New England families had migrated into what was to become lower Canada decades before the conflict with England. Since they were living in the "Colonies", there was no particular separation between families, cousins, etc.

A further complication came about when the British Crown sold land to citizens of the new country as early as 1795, in an effort to develop the wilderness of what is now Quebec. Families south of the border had prospered and increased to the point where it was necessary to acquire more land so that younger sons could have their farms nearby to their fathers and grandfathers.

Soon there were many settlers in lower Canada of English descent in an area known as the "Eastern Townships". So it was that many families who had patriotically supported the War for Independence had close ties in lower Quebec. The heavily

French-dominated area was not at all discouraging to them, even though they were not Roman Catholics and never converted to that faith. The only restriction placed upon them that life events, baptism, marriage and burial, required recording by a Notary according to a pre-determined protocol. Beyond that, they were free to have their own churches and cemeteries and follow their own faiths. Indeed, many of the towns in that area had English names such as Compton, Stanstead, etc.

As a result, the War of 1812 for many of these families was at best an interruption to their daily lives. They cared little for the political posturing of governments, and the possibility of British attack was not even a reality for them. News of the conflicts and their horrors were delayed in reaching them and very likely watered down once that it got there. Theirs was a hardscrabble life. Daily survival was paramount. And they had no stomach for fighting their friends, neighbors, and cousins. This is not to say that they did not support their country and its survival, but rather to observe that they did not have the same view of the peril. Certainly their neighbors to the north were not any danger to them. Had they wished to participate, it would have been nearly impossible to do so.

Not only was it difficult to get to the far-away battlefields across areas inhospitable to travel, but they did not observe the danger to be as severe as others might have seen it. And someone would have to take care of the farm while they were gone. This was a tall order as the involvement of every member of the family was essential to the process. Added to this confusion was the fact that the Canadian government exercised an uneven attitude towards citizens "north" of Vermont. Occasionally they were called to service, and even a draft was proposed, with little success. An embargo against the "import" of foreign goods (i.e, from the U.S.) was set up and largely ignored. Similar neglect occurred "south" of the border. Citizens on both sides depended on trade across the border for daily living. Embargos on the part of both governments were largely ignored, and "smuggling" was rampant as the daily necessities of life traveled both ways across the border.

So, life went on for these citizens, and little did they dream that their conduct of their daily lives in the early nineteenth century would lead to such a frustration on my part in the early 21st century.

EPILOGUE

Epilogue:

The National Society Daughters of the American Revolution, founded in 1890 and headquartered in Washington, D.C., is a non-profit, non-political volunteer women's service organization dedicated to promoting patriotism, preserving American history, and securing America's future through better education of children. Founded on October 11, 1890 by a group of four pioneering women, it was their belief that to express their patriotic feelings there was a need for a women's organization to perpetuate the memory of ancestors who fought to make this country free and independent.

Rainier Chapter was organized on September 20, 1895 and received its National Charter number of 155 on December 13, 1895. The original membership was comprised of twenty Seattle members and the meetings took place in the members' homes. Within ten years the membership had grown to over 200 women and the monthly meetings were conducted in the larger hotels, notably the Lincoln Hotel. As the city expanded, so did the interest in DAR. Throughout the first part of the 20th Century, new Washington State Chapters were formed by Rainier Chapter members to accommodate the needs of the local membership.

In 1908 the members were approached by Professor Edmund Meany to participate in the funding of the placement of a permanent statue of George Washington on the campus of the Alaska Yukon Pacific Exposition. The successful solicitation of funds from school children, the SAR and prominent community leaders resulted in the commission of a statue by Loredo Taft, a noted Chicago sculptor. The statue was dedicated on June 14, 1909 and was rededicated in 2009.

In 1920 it became apparent that the membership was in need of a permanent Chapter House. A building committee was formed and land was purchased in 1922. Fundraising commenced and with the selling of building bonds, the construction of the Rainier Chapter House was started in January of 1925. The Chapter House was completed in April of 1925. The Chapter House was purposely built to serve the membership and to enable the members to carry out the tenants of the National Society: Historic Preservation, Service to Veterans, Education. But from the first month of operation the Chapter House was also offered for rental to the general public so that the citizens of Seattle could enjoy and use the facility.

Rainier Chapter House

During World War II, the Rainier Chapter members donated space in the Chapter House for use by the American Red Cross. Members also held fundraisers and with the proceeds going to entertain servicemen. In 1976 Rainier Chapter participated in many Bicentennial programs and handed out over 2,500 American flag history pamphlets. Each year Rainier Chapter participates in the Naturalization Ceremony for new American citizens held at the Seattle Center. During the last ten years, Rainier Chapter members have given generously and have awarded many scholarships to both men and women seeking higher education.

Rainier Chapter's members are a reflection of their community and are today's representatives of the Rainier Chapter legacy. Over one hundred years have passed since the formation of Rainier Chapter and over 2,000 women have participated and been part of the Rainier Chapter. The current members are passionate about their family history and the contributions their ancestors made to the formation of our country. Because our National Society encourages and supports participation in so many areas of interest (i.e. the study of American history, American arts, Native American culture, scholarship awards, service to veterans) Rainier Chapter has a vibrant and active Chapter.

www.ingramcontent.com/pod-product-compliance
Ingram Content Group UK Ltd.
Pitfield, Milton Keynes, MK11 3LW, UK
UKHW041941190726
13854UKWH00004B/1725

9 781105 732317